Bettina Wohlgemuth-Fekonja

öbv

Prime Time 5

Testen und Fördern

www.oebv.at

Liebe Schülerin, lieber Schüler!

Dieses Heft enthält **Tests** zu den Bereichen *Listening*, *Reading*, *Language in use* und *Writing*. Im Anschluss daran finden Sie **Förderhinweise** mit Verweisen auf passende Stellen in Ihrem *Coursebook*.

Die **Lösungen** finden Sie gesammelt am Ende des Buches. Dieser Bereich enthält auch Informationen zu den jeweils überprüften **Kompetenzen**.

Die Audio-Dateien, die Sie für die *Listening*-Aufgaben brauchen, finden Sie über einen

Online-Code auf der Website www.oebv.at.

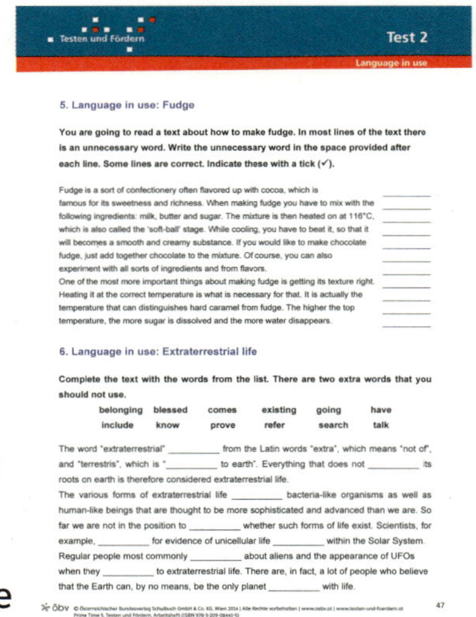

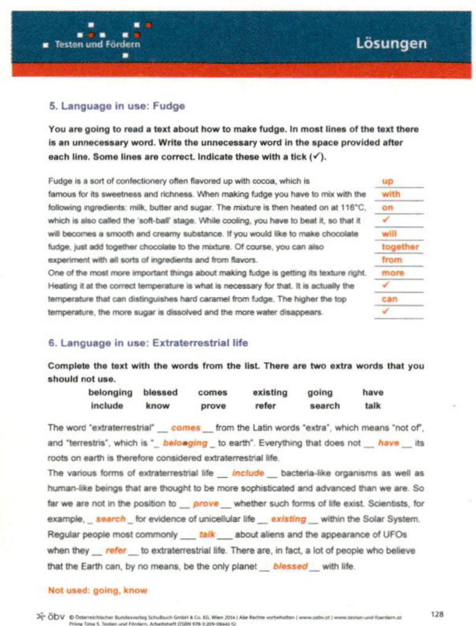

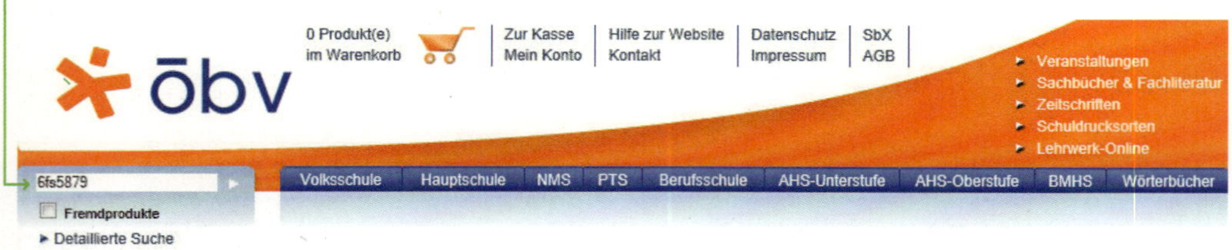

Hinweis für Lehrerinnen und Lehrer

Auf www.testen-und-foerdern.at finden Sie die abgedruckten Tests auch als interaktive Anwendungen.

Haben Ihre Schülerinnen und Schüler die Tests bearbeitet, erhalten Sie eine Auswertung nach verschiedenen Kompetenzbereichen für die gesamte Klasse und individuell für jeden Schüler und jede Schülerin. Förderhinweise verweisen auf jeweils passende Stellen im *Coursebook*.

Nähere Informationen zum Onlineportal Testen-und-Fördern finden Sie auch auf www.oebv.at und auf www.testen-und-foerdern.at.

Inhaltsverzeichnis

Prime Time 5. Testen und Fördern, Arbeitsheft (ISBN 978-3-209-08441-5)

Prime Time 5. Testen und Fördern, Arbeitsheft (ISBN 978-3-209-08441-5)

1. Listening: Actionwork

You will hear part of a radio programme in which Brian Williams interviews Roanna Burton about 'Actionwork'. For questions 1–5, choose the answer which fits best according to what you hear.

1. What audience does TOLF address?

- ☐ adults in their 30s
- ☐ teenagers
- ☐ elderly people

2. What media does 'Actionwork' use to promote its ideas?

- ☐ print media
- ☐ radio and the Internet
- ☐ movies and plays

3. Since when has 'Actionwork' been active?

- ☐ since 1919
- ☐ since 2003
- ☐ since 1990

Prime Time 5. Testen und Fördern, Arbeitsheft (ISBN 978-3-209-08441-5)

4. 'Actionwork' deals with a lot of different problems. Which of these problems is NOT mentioned in the interview?

- ☐ cyber bullying
- ☐ peer pressure
- ☐ illegal substances

5. In how far my bullying change the victims' character?

- ☐ They may turn aggressive later in life.
- ☐ They may become self-centered and selfish people.
- ☐ They may be frightened and stop trusting themselves.

Prime Time 5. Testen und Fördern, Arbeitsheft (ISBN 978-3-209-08441-5)

2. Listening: Mike Baker

You will hear part of a radio report in which Mike Baker talks about his career as a ski jumper. For statements 1–6, choose the correct answer (True or False) which fits best according to what you hear.

1. School kept Mike very busy.

- ☐ True
- ☐ False

2. Skiing fascinated him from the very beginning.

- ☐ True
- ☐ False

3. His uncle was a ski jumper himself.

- ☐ True
- ☐ False

Prime Time 5. Testen und Fördern, Arbeitsheft (ISBN 978-3-209-08441-5)

4. Mike had to stop ski jumping for 2 years because his family moved to another city.

- ☐ True
- ☐ False

5. While he attended the National Sport School, he had the chance to travel a lot.

- ☐ True
- ☐ False

6. He will definitely take part in the next Winter Olympics.

- ☐ True
- ☐ False

Prime Time 5. Testen und Fördern, Arbeitsheft (ISBN 978-3-209-08441-5)

3. Reading: How to improve your performance at school

You are going to read a text on improving your performance at school. For questions 1–5, choose the answer which fits best according to what you read.

At the beginning of a new school year many students plan on doing better at school than the year before. While they are very motivated at first, they often do not know how to get good grades in the long run. Here's a list of the most useful strategies.

Be active in all your classes. While it is very important to attend your classes regularly and pay attention to what your teachers say, it is even more important to actively participate in what is going on. Ask questions, make it known if you don't understand something, take part in class discussions, and share your experiences and opinions with your classmates and teachers.

Take good notes. Being able to take good notes is vital not only at school but also at work later on. It starts with being a good listener who is able to identify the most important information. Key points and definitions as well as diagrams should be noted down. Since you are busy during the lesson and do not have that much time to revise your notes, make sure you take a second look at them at home. Re-write them if necessary. A good structure can help you a great deal as soon as you have to study the material.

Master your teachers. You have probably noticed already that every teacher has their own style of teaching and system of grading. It is important to keep that in mind when preparing for any kind of exam and doing your homework. Make sure you know what they want and try to meet their expectations. Communicating with them is important too. Remember that they are also people who sometimes have problems understanding something. If you let them know that you are struggling, they might be able to help.

Be organized. You should not only organize your notes but also your daily schedule. Keep a diary on exam dates and homework assignments as well as presentations and papers. Plan enough time to prepare for all of them and do not try to do five different things at one time. It helps to concentrate on the more difficult things first and keep the easier ones for later. If you use your time wisely, it definitely pays off later on. You can then avoid feeling stressed and do your school work one step at a time. Still don't forget to take breaks on a regular basis.

Be a good test-taker. Your grades depend to a great extent on getting good results on exams. If you have known your teacher for a while you should know what to expect. For new teachers you could try to get copies of old tests and exams. Go to the test well-prepared …… ……. you can relax and completely focus on the tasks presented to you. Read the instructions carefully and ask any questions you might have before the test begins. It's crucial that you really understand what you have to do to perform well on the tasks. Normally you don't get the same number of points for each task, so make sure you do the ones with the highest number of points first.

Stick to our suggestions and you will improve your grades for sure! ☺

Prime Time 5. Testen und Fördern, Arbeitsheft (ISBN 978-3-209-08441-5)

1. According to the text, what is the most important thing you should do to be active in your classes?

- ☐ go to your classes regularly
- ☐ be attentive at all times
- ☐ learn how to listen
- ☐ take part in the lesson

2. Why should you have another look at your notes after the lesson?

- ☐ to include diagrams and definitions
- ☐ to check whether you have written down everything
- ☐ to structure and organize your notes well
- ☐ to write them down a second time

3. "Be organized. […] If you use your time wisely, it definitely pays off later on. […]"
What is the meaning of the phrase "to pay off" in this context?

- ☐ You are in a better situation later on.
- ☐ You have to do several things at a time later on.
- ☐ You are more stressed out later on.
- ☐ You have nothing to do later on.

Prime Time 5. Testen und Fördern, Arbeitsheft (ISBN 978-3-209-08441-5)

4. **"Be a good test-taker.** […] Go to the test well-prepared …… …… you can relax and completely focus on the tasks presented to you."
Two words are missing in the text. Choose the words that fit best.

- ☐ because so
- ☐ so that
- ☐ for that
- ☐ then so

5. Who is this text written for?

- ☐ students who have problems with their teachers
- ☐ students who want to learn how to take notes
- ☐ students who want to do well at school
- ☐ students who have problems at home because of school

Prime Time 5. Testen und Fördern, Arbeitsheft (ISBN 978-3-209-08441-5)

4. Reading: Worlds apart

You are going to read two texts about computers and the Internet. For statements 1–8, choose the answer (True, False or Not given) which fits best according to what you read.

ATSU "Most people in my country do not have a computer of their own. For starters, it's not exactly cheap to buy and maintain one. Compared to Western countries, the ones you get here are quite expensive. I bought mine, which is a rather big one, about a year ago as a second-hand computer. Around here in Mozambique you don't get to see a lot of iPads or netbooks. Second, access to the Internet can be problematic. I, for example, have to get up around 4 in the morning if I want to have reliable and fast service. Access happens via dial-up and as soon as there is a great number of people surfing the net at the same time the connection slows down dramatically. Even under the best conditions I have to keep in mind my 128Kbps bandwidth. For those who do not have Internet access at home or who cannot afford a computer in the first place, cyber cafés have become extremely popular places. Even I sometimes use them. As a journalist I depend on Internet access to be informed about what is happening around the world. Web logs in particular are very useful because they allow news to travel fast and reach lots of different people."

YON "We have seven computers at home. Two of them are mine, my husband has two as well and each of our three kids has their own. I prefer using the laptop when travelling; at home I usually work on the desktop.

Life without a computer or Internet access would be impossible for me. I have been using and working on the computer for about two decades now and I am amazed at the incredible developments in terms of size, RAM and speed at which data can be processed. Especially at work the computer comes in very handy when accessing all sorts of information and contacting people. There is no longer any need to rifle through files and I can provide my boss with up-to-date figures and numbers within minutes. At home I generally use the computer to stay in touch with family and friends. My son spends most of his time playing online games. My younger daughter uses hers for educational purposes, and our youngest loves chat rooms and social networks. While seven computers in one household may be an exception in other countries, it's typical for a South Korean family. Here lots of people have computers and a quarter of all inhabitants use high-speed Internet."

Prime Time 5. Testen und Fördern, Arbeitsheft (ISBN 978-3-209-08441-5)

1. In Mozambique you cannot buy iPads or netbooks.

- ☐ True
- ☐ False
- ☐ Not given

2. To use the Internet in Mozambique you must get up at 4.

- ☐ True
- ☐ False
- ☐ Not given

3. The connection gets worse when more people are online.

- ☐ True
- ☐ False
- ☐ Not given

4. Journalists frequently use cyber cafés.

- ☐ True
- ☐ False
- ☐ Not given

Prime Time 5. Testen und Fördern, Arbeitsheft (ISBN 978-3-209-08441-5)

5. Yon says that the laptop is easier to use on a trip.

- ☐ True
- ☐ False
- ☐ Not given

6. She exclusively uses the computer to stay in contact with business partners.

- ☐ True
- ☐ False
- ☐ Not given

7. None of her children use the computer for school.

- ☐ True
- ☐ False
- ☐ Not given

8. 25% of all people in South Korea have high-speed Internet access.

- ☐ True
- ☐ False
- ☐ Not given

Prime Time 5. Testen und Fördern, Arbeitsheft (ISBN 978-3-209-08441-5)

5. Writing: An argument (Diary entry)

You have just had an argument with one of your parents. Both of you got very angry and upset. You are now in your room. To calm down you write about the conflict in your diary.

Make sure to include the following points:

- how the conflict began
- what it was about
- how it stopped
- what you are planning to do next

Prime Time 5. Testen und Fördern, Arbeitsheft (ISBN 978-3-209-08441-5)

1. Listening: Catching up on the phone

You will hear a telephone conversation in which George talks to Emily. For questions 1–5, choose the answer that fits best according to what you hear.

1. Where did Emily do her internship?

- ☐ England
- ☐ Scotland
- ☐ Wales
- ☐ Ireland

2. What do you learn about Sarah's job situation?

- ☐ She wants to change jobs.
- ☐ She wants to work for another company.
- ☐ She is very unhappy with her old job.
- ☐ She is about to get a promotion.

Prime Time 5. Testen und Fördern, Arbeitsheft (ISBN 978-3-209-08441-5)

3. What does George think about his son's new hobby?

- ☐ He is impressed by his son's talent.
- ☐ He refuses to pay for his son's guitar lessons.
- ☐ He thinks that his son needs to practise.
- ☐ He is sure his son will be a rockstar soon.

4. What is Emily's opinion about Mary's relationship?

- ☐ She thinks that there is no reason to worry.
- ☐ She thinks that Mary should be more responsible.
- ☐ She thinks that George should not accept it.
- ☐ She thinks that Mary is still too young.

5. According to the conversation, who is Sarah?

- ☐ George's sister
- ☐ Emily's best friend
- ☐ Emily's sister
- ☐ George's wife

Prime Time 5. Testen und Fördern, Arbeitsheft (ISBN 978-3-209-08441-5)

2. Listening: Today's fashion designers

You will hear part of a podcast in which Alyssa talks about today's fashion designers. For statements 1–6, choose the answer (True or False) that fits best according to what you hear.

1. The programme is called UCF podcasts.

- ☐ True
- ☐ False

2. Pop stars have not always decided what is fashionable.

- ☐ True
- ☐ False

3. Sheryl can afford designer clothes.

- ☐ True
- ☐ False

Prime Time 5. Testen und Fördern, Arbeitsheft (ISBN 978-3-209-08441-5)

4. Celebrities design their own clothes because they want their fans to feel more like them.

☐ True

☐ False

5. More and more pop stars worry that they will not stay popular for a long time.

☐ True

☐ False

6. The report explains the importance of stars in fashion.

☐ True

☐ False

Prime Time 5. Testen und Fördern, Arbeitsheft (ISBN 978-3-209-08441-5)

3. Reading: Less sugar in Kellogg's cereals

You are going to read a text about a change in Kellogg's cereals. For statements 1–7, choose the answer (True, False or Not given) which fits best according to what you read.

Kellogg's is reacting to several claims that cereals, which show high levels of sugar, salt and fat, can contribute to childhood obesity. Kellogg's UK managing director Greg Peterson says that they are more than willing to act upon lots of mothers' wishes for tasty cereals with low sugar content. Changing four of Kellogg's Coco Pops products in the next year will be the first step towards a future of healthier cereals.

At the moment Coco Pops contain about 35% sugar. Having invested a lot of money and staff hours in the course of the past two years, Kellogg's will soon manage to reduce the sugar content to approximately 29%, which will, however, still be almost twice the amount recommended by the Food Standards Agency.

Lucy Jones, a member of the British Dietetic Association, confirms that Kellogg's has at least made a small move in the right direction and by doing so is clearly following a trend of sugar, salt and fat reductions in food. Salt levels in particular have fallen a great deal in various products in the past few years. However, Jones also points out that further reductions in sugar will be necessary in the future since sugar does not only affect the people's weight management but also their teeth and blood glucose levels.

With Kellogg's being among the most popular cereal producers, many parents appreciate this change in the quality of Kellogg's products. In the UK, for example, four out of ten people have at least one box of Coco Pops at home. Considering nutritionists' claim that breakfast is the most important meal of the day, health-conscious parents who want their children to have breakfast are, naturally, eager to put something healthy and at the same time tasty on the table.

Several studies have proven the importance of having breakfast. Starting the day without it can have a negative influence on people's concentration and energy levels and, in the long run, also lead to weight problems.

Greg Peterson has confirmed Kellogg's' intention to keep reducing sugar levels in the future if they can maintain the quality of the product taste.

Prime Time 5. Testen und Fördern, Arbeitsheft (ISBN 978-3-209-08441-5)

1. Kellogg's will reduce the sugar content of all Kellogg's Coco Pops products in the next year.

- ☐ True
- ☐ False
- ☐ Not given

2. Kellogg's spent a small amount of money on the product's quality.

- ☐ True
- ☐ False
- ☐ Not given

3. The Food Standards Agency does not recommend Kellogg's products.

- ☐ True
- ☐ False
- ☐ Not given

4. Lucy Jones welcomes the changes Kellogg's has made.

- ☐ True
- ☐ False
- ☐ Not given

Prime Time 5. Testen und Fördern, Arbeitsheft (ISBN 978-3-209-08441-5)

5. According to the text, high sugar levels only cause weight problems.

☐ True

☐ False

☐ Not given

6. 40% of all consumers in the UK buy Kellogg's products.

☐ True

☐ False

☐ Not given

7. People usually are in a better mood after having breakfast.

☐ True

☐ False

☐ Not given

Prime Time 5. Testen und Fördern, Arbeitsheft (ISBN 978-3-209-08441-5)

4. Reading: Summer Jobs

You are going to read a text on summer jobs. For questions 1–5, choose the answer that fits best according to what you read.

During the summer holidays a lot of teenagers decide to take on a job. As soon as you reach the age of 15, you have the permission to work in your holidays. Going to work means taking over new responsibilities, following orders and also getting up early, which does not always appeal to young people. However, summer jobs have attractive benefits. After learning about the following three reasons for getting yourself a job we are sure you will want to go out and find one.

Work experience

Summer jobs are a great opportunity to get to know various work fields. Acquiring useful skills and gaining knowledge about all sorts of working processes is only one of many advantages. If you realize that the line of work you have chosen is not the right one for you, just remember that the time you spend at a summer job is limited. Finding out about your likes and dislikes will help you plan your future. In addition to the work experience, you also get the chance to work on your self-confidence and feel good about yourself.

Teamwork

No matter whether you work at a gas station, in an office or a supermarket, you always work together with other people. Working in a team can be a challenge because you cannot only think about your own needs, you also have to accept the opinions of others. You must be ready to share your ideas, help others out and show understanding for your fellow colleagues. Today being able to work in a team often decides whether you get a job or not.

Money

Another very attractive advantage of spending your summer holidays working is the money you earn. In Austria teenagers usually make between 600 and 1,000 Euros per month. Making your own money gives you a feeling of independence from your parents. In addition, you can afford bigger expenses like paying for your driver's license or a new computer.

Of course, you could spend your holidays sitting on the couch at home, playing computer games or watching TV all day long but this will not get you anywhere. So write your application, go to the interview, get the job and set your alarm: It's time to leave for work and conquer the world.

Prime Time 5. Testen und Fördern, Arbeitsheft (ISBN 978-3-209-08441-5)

1. Why do teenagers only start doing summer jobs at the age of 15?

- ☐ Younger teenagers are not responsible enough before that.
- ☐ Younger teenagers do not want to get up that early.
- ☐ Younger teenagers are not allowed to take a job.

2. Why is it sometimes good that summer jobs only last for a few weeks?

- ☐ Because you learn new things very quickly.
- ☐ Because you might have to do something you don't like.
- ☐ Because you can still enjoy part of your holiday.

3. What makes working in a team a challenge?

- ☐ Your needs are less important than your colleagues' needs.
- ☐ You should be willing to deal with other people's views.
- ☐ You always have to come up with new ideas.

Prime Time 5. Testen und Fördern, Arbeitsheft (ISBN 978-3-209-08441-5)

4. According to the text, what is meant by the word "expenses"?

- ☐ the money you save
- ☐ the money you earn
- ☐ the money you spend

5. What do the authors of this text want you to do?

- ☐ get work experience
- ☐ earn a lot of money
- ☐ plan your future

5. Writing: Exchanging experiences (Letter)

Your British penfriend has written you a letter, telling you a little bit about his/her school and what a typical day at school looks like. You have decided to write him/her a letter in which you describe your own school and your life as a pupil.

Make sure to include the following points:

- how long you are at school every day
- how many different subjects you have
- if you wear a school uniform and what you think about it
- what you like best and what you don't like about school

Prime Time 5. Testen und Fördern, Arbeitsheft (ISBN 978-3-209-08441-5)

1. Listening: Boys at school

You will hear part of a radio interview with 15-year-old Bill about school. For questions 1–5, choose the answer which fits best according to what you hear.

1. What have recent studies shown?

- ☐ Girls are as good as boys at school.
- ☐ Boys do better at school than girls.
- ☐ Girls produce better results than boys.

2. When will the School Improvement Officer be on air?

- ☐ the next day
- ☐ later that day
- ☐ some time next week

Prime Time 5. Testen und Fördern, Arbeitsheft (ISBN 978-3-209-08441-5)

3. In secondary school, how did Bill deal with his workload?

☐ He did not work hard enough.

☐ He gave up quickly.

☐ He tried to manage the pressure.

4. How did his bad marks affect his opinion about school?

☐ They did not affect his opinion at all.

☐ He started to dislike school.

☐ He was annoyed by his teachers' reaction.

5. Was Bill the only boy in his class with problems?

☐ There were a few boys facing the same problems.

☐ Bill was the one having the biggest problems.

☐ Most of the boys in his class had the same problems.

Prime Time 5. Testen und Fördern, Arbeitsheft (ISBN 978-3-209-08441-5)

2. Listening: Hip hop

You will hear part of a radio interview about hip hop. For statements 1–7, choose the answer (True or False) which fits best according to what you hear.

1. The radio guest's name is Karen Easton.

☐ True

☐ False

2. Hip hop started in one particular area of New York City.

☐ True

☐ False

3. In hip hop five stylistic elements are mixed together.

☐ True

☐ False

Prime Time 5. Testen und Fördern, Arbeitsheft (ISBN 978-3-209-08441-5)

4. Hip hop is not the same as rap.

- ☐ True
- ☐ False

5. A lot of music genres come from African music.

- ☐ True
- ☐ False

6. The radio guest Karen is not coming back after the break.

- ☐ True
- ☐ False

7. The people at block parties liked funk and soul music.

- ☐ True
- ☐ False

Prime Time 5. Testen und Fördern, Arbeitsheft (ISBN 978-3-209-08441-5)

3. Reading: Package holidays

You are going to read a text on package holidays. For questions 1–5, choose the answer which fits best according to what you read.

Package holidays

Package holidays, also known as package tours, are a holiday combination of transport and accommodation generally geared toward travelers favoring mass tourism. These package holidays usually include services like a rental car or different sorts of activities or trips during the holidays. They are generally organized by tour operators, and marketed and sold to consumers by travel agents. While some travel agents work for tour operators, others are independent.

In the majority of cases, tourists make use of charter airlines to travel to foreign countries. Flights provided on a charter basis are generally more expensive but at the same time more convenient for travelers because they operate outside normal schedules.

Thomas Cook was the first person to offer a package tour of Europe in 1855 after organizing what could be considered an early form of package holiday in 1841, namely a return trip between Leicester and Loughborough. By the beginning of the 1870s, Cook was in the position to offer tours all over the world, but only for small groups of tourists.

Vladimir Raitz, co-founder of the Horizon Holiday Group and father of the modern British package holiday, pioneered mass package holidays abroad via charter airlines. In 1950, he offered an all-inclusive holiday in Corsica, departing from Gatwick airport. Eleven paying customers took part in his inaugural flight and enjoyed a holiday consisting of a return ticket, tented accommodation on the beach and tasty food.

At the time, a return flight to Nice, for instance, was £70, the equivalent of approximately £1.700 these days. In the 1960s, only ten years after the first mass package holiday had been offered, more and more people in the UK could afford to travel abroad, always enjoying a well-prepared combination of flight, transfers and accommodation.

At the beginning of the twenty-first century, travelers started avoiding package holidays and concentrating on traveling with budget airlines and taking care of their accommodation themselves. In the UK, the decline in package holidays resulted in the consolidation of the tour operator market, which is now ruled by a few big tour operators, including Thomson Holidays, Thomas Cook AG and First Choice.

As a considerable number of flight and holiday companies filed for bankruptcy and the hidden costs of no-frills flights – such as extra charge for heavy baggage or check-in at the airport instead of online check-in – kept increasing, travelers wanted financial security, which helped package holidays see a new boost in 2009. An increase in last-minute bookings has also made package holidays more popular again.

Prime Time 5. Testen und Fördern, Arbeitsheft (ISBN 978-3-209-08441-5)

1. What role do travel agents play with regard to package holidays?

- ☐ They exclusively work for tour operators.
- ☐ They organize package holidays.
- ☐ They offer package holidays.

2. What is the main benefit of charter flights?

- ☐ They are more flexible.
- ☐ They follow normal schedules.
- ☐ They are cheaper.

3. "Vladimir Raitz [...] pioneered mass package holidays abroad via charter airlines." What does "*pioneer*" mean in this context?

- ☐ He was the first to transport package holiday travelers.
- ☐ He was the first to offer all-inclusive holidays.
- ☐ He was the first to organize package holidays for large groups.

4. What led to a decrease in package holidays at the beginning of the new millennium?

- ☐ The market was controlled by a small number of big tour operators.
- ☐ Tourists took more action in organizing their own holidays.
- ☐ The number of budget airlines offering cheap flights increased.

Prime Time 5. Testen und Fördern, Arbeitsheft (ISBN 978-3-209-08441-5)

5. Why did travelers return to booking package holidays a few years later?

☐ Because many holiday companies and airlines closed down.

☐ Because package holidays had become cheaper.

☐ Because package holidays did not produce additional costs.

Prime Time 5. Testen und Fördern, Arbeitsheft (ISBN 978-3-209-08441-5)

4. Reading: Eating disorders in teenagers

You are going to read a text on eating disorders in teenagers. For statements 1–6, choose the answer (True or False) which fits best according to what you read.

Eating disorders in teenagers

With the onset of puberty, children turn into teenagers and a period called adolescence begins. Adolescence is the time between puberty and young adulthood, in which the young human body undergoes important physical and mental changes.

To form the basis for normal development and growth, teenagers do not only need constant support, understanding and time to reflect on themselves and their actions, but also a lot of healthy high-quality food. Their bones grow quickly and, depending on the teenagers' growing needs, they should consume high calorie foods.

In Western society in particular, more and more teenagers harm their bodies instead of taking good care of them. One problem a great number of teenagers but also young adults are facing today are eating disorders, which affect the human body negatively. Eating disorders are now considered the third most common chronic disease, especially in young women. The number of people affected has been rising dramatically in the past three decades. If not treated as early as possible, complex illnesses may be a consequence.

An eating disorder, in general, is a condition characterised by abnormal eating behaviour that may involve either too little or too much food intake. While there are quite a number of different eating disorders, anorexia nervosa and bulimia nervosa are the most common ones in young people.

People who starve themselves suffer from anorexia nervosa. The weight loss such people experience is extreme and normally 15% below their normal body weight. The main problem with anorexic people is that, regardless of how thin they are, they always believe that they are too fat. Their fear of gaining weight makes them do excessive exercise, take in laxatives or refuse to eat at all.

Bulimia nervosa is an eating disorder characterised by a combination of refusing to eat and taking in loads of food in a very short period of time. Feelings of guilt, weakness and low self-esteem are often the result of excessive food intake. In order to compensate for these bad feelings, bulimic people try to get rid of the food they have eaten, either by throwing up or by using laxatives.

Teenagers suffering from eating disorders frequently have to deal with serious medical consequences, such as growth retardation, abnormal weight and pubertal delay. Girls in particular have to face irregular or even absent menstruation. Eating disorders can also lead to a loss of body fat, muscle mass as well as bone mineral when the human body is growing. Moreover, there might be abnormalities with regard to one's levels of vitamins, minerals and other trace elements. These problems do not go away when entering adulthood. In fact, they get worse.

Apart from the medical consequences, eating disorders go hand in hand with psychological and emotional problems. People, especially teenagers, suffering from eating disorders often isolate themselves. They also fall easy victim to feelings of anxiety, low self-worth and depression. Regardless of whether one addresses the physical or the psychological consequences of eating disorders, both of them are destructive and affect people's quality of life extremely negatively.

Prime Time 5. Testen und Fördern, Arbeitsheft (ISBN 978-3-209-08441-5)

1. Teenagers should avoid meals with a high calorie count.

- ☐ True
- ☐ False

2. The amount of people suffering from eating disorders is slowly increasing.

- ☐ True
- ☐ False

3. An eating disorder is connected to an excessive intake of food.

- ☐ True
- ☐ False

4. Anorexic people have a wrong image of their own body.

- ☐ True
- ☐ False

5. People suffering from eating disorders have more problems the older they get.

- ☐ True
- ☐ False

6. Bulimic and anorexic people often turn away from social contacts.

- ☐ True
- ☐ False

Prime Time 5. Testen und Fördern, Arbeitsheft (ISBN 978-3-209-08441-5)

5. Language in use: Job interviews

Read the text on job interviews. Some words are missing. Use the words in brackets to form words that fit in the gaps. Write your answers in the gaps.

When .... (**prepare**) for a job interview, you need to know what the company is looking for. Interviewers want to employ people who are intelligent, flexible and able to work in a team. It is also important to be good at .... (**communicate**) with others and expressing yourself .... (**clear**).

.... (**Apply**) for a job are usually asked about their work experience and their education. Take every chance to gain .... (**know**) about the field you plan on working in. Summer jobs and unpaid internships often pay off later on.

Before going to the .... (**actual**) interview, make sure to do your research. You should know what the company does and who the most important people like managers and supervisors are. Moreover, think about what to wear. It is always good to be .... (**dress**) smartly.

6. Language in use: Dear diary

Read the diary entry and choose the correct preposition for each gap. Write it in the gap.

Dear diary,

today has been the worst day .... (**from / of / in**) my life. You know Mary, my best friend. We have known each other .... (**over / since / for**) ages and we have never really had a fight before. Up till now! She did the most horrible thing .... (**to / for / at**) me that you can imagine. She really had the nerve to flirt .... (**about / with / at**) Tony, even though she knows that I am secretly in love .... (**toward / with / for**) him.

I had just entered the cafeteria when I saw them standing close .... (**next / around / to**) each other. I left without asking them what they were talking .... (**over / about / through**). I don't want to see her tomorrow! What if …

Prime Time 5. Testen und Fördern, Arbeitsheft (ISBN 978-3-209-08441-5)

7. Writing: On holiday in Malta (Blog entry)

You are on holiday in Malta with your parents. To keep your friends updated, you decide to write a blog entry of about 190 words and post it on your homepage describing your experiences so far.

Make sure to include the following points:

- arrival and trip to the hotel
- weather
- description of the hotel and food
- activities

Prime Time 5. Testen und Fördern, Arbeitsheft (ISBN 978-3-209-08441-5)

Fertigkeit	Aufgabe in Testen und Fördern	Entsprechung in Schülerbuch Prime Time 5	Seite
Listening	*Boys at School (MC)*	Now that's what I call living (1–8)	
		1+2 Read the following text from a British novel about a boy's biography. (**taking notes + answering questions**)	21
		4 Read the text now and highlight passages that explain what type of person Jimmy is.	22
		6 Examine the text structure.	23
		7 Complete the sentences about Jimmy's early life.	23
		8 Make up Jimmy's answers.	23
Listening	*Hip Hop (T/F)*	**2** A job in a sports shop. (**taking notes + questions**)	122
		4 The future of print media. (**MC 1aus 4**)	137
Reading	*Package holidays (MC)*	**2+3** Going home – When and where? Read the story and highlight passages that refer to times and locations. (**questions**)	76f.

Prime Time 5. Testen und Fördern, Arbeitsheft (ISBN 978-3-209-08441-5)

Fertigkeit	Aufgabe in Testen und Fördern	Entsprechung in Schülerbuch Prime Time 5	Seite
Reading	*Eating disorders in teenagers (T/F)*	**1–3** Producing your own music. (**open**)	100f.
		1–3 More teens moving away from CDs (**questions**)	109
LiU	*Job interviews (word formation)*	**4** Sylvia's new job. You are going to read a text about Sylvia's new job. Some words are missing from the text. (**gap-filling**)	43
LiU	*Dear diary (prepositions: gap-filling)*	**3** Blake's Barbie: let, make, have. (**gap-filling**)	39
		4 Let, make or have – Complete the sentences. (**gap-filling**)	39

Prime Time 5. Testen und Fördern, Arbeitsheft (ISBN 978-3-209-08441-5)

1. Listening: The Maitreya Project in India

You will hear part of a radio interview between Eric Clark and Bita Rina on the Maitreya Education Project in India. For questions 1-5, choose the answer which fits best according to what you hear.

1. What is Bita Rina's role in the Maitreya Project?

- ☐ She is a sponsor.
- ☐ She is the founder.
- ☐ She is a representative.

2. What does the project NOT focus on?

- ☐ healthcare
- ☐ social welfare
- ☐ infrastructure

3. Why is the project of great importance for that region?

- ☐ Because most people are unemployed.
- ☐ Because most people are badly educated.
- ☐ Because most people need better medical treatment.

Prime Time 5. Testen und Fördern, Arbeitsheft (ISBN 978-3-209-08441-5)

4. Under what condition will new schools be built?

- ☐ Sponsors provide both money and locations.
- ☐ There is a higher interest of children and adults in education.
- ☐ The curriculum covers a greater variety of subjects.

5. What is the "good heart"?

- ☐ a subject
- ☐ a project
- ☐ a concept

Prime Time 5. Testen und Fördern, Arbeitsheft (ISBN 978-3-209-08441-5)

2. Listening: Mice

You will hear a radio report about mice. For statements 1-7, choose the answer (True or False) which fits best according to what you hear.

1. The field mouse is the best-known mouse species.

☐ True

☐ False

2. Despite their many natural enemies, mice can live in nearly all areas.

☐ True

☐ False

3. Mice are carriers of illnesses.

☐ True

☐ False

Prime Time 5. Testen und Fördern, Arbeitsheft (ISBN 978-3-209-08441-5)

4. Mice are most active during the day.

- ☐ True
- ☐ False

5. Mice can see as well as they can hear.

- ☐ True
- ☐ False

6. Mice are often used in labs although they are expensive.

- ☐ True
- ☐ False

7. Mice easily adapt around humans.

- ☐ True
- ☐ False

Prime Time 5. Testen und Fördern, Arbeitsheft (ISBN 978-3-209-08441-5)

3. Reading: The importance of reading

You are going to read a text on the importance of reading. For questions 1-5, choose the answer which fits best according to what you read.

The importance of reading

Being able to read is one of the most valuable skills to be acquired because it opens the doors to infinite knowledge and changes our view of the world and of the people who live in it. The skill of reading therefore plays an important role in an individual's personal and educational development.

Although used throughout in education, more and more people do not consider reading a pleasant free-time activity. For young people especially, reading often becomes an imposition, something that they would like to avoid if at all possible. One reason for people losing interest in reading is the availability of all sorts of media which seem to be far more attractive these days because they often do not ask for being active. A growing number of young people, children and teenagers alike, prefer spending their time playing computer games or watching television. Adults often busy themselves with work or seemingly more exciting leisure time activities too.

People who understand the importance of reading keep pointing out how crucial it is that we do not stop reading but that we learn to appreciate the benefit of it. Children in particular need to be made familiar with books and their advantages from an early age.

There are various reasons why reading is of high significance to us. Children who are read to – or read themselves as soon as they are able to – develop a greater ability of understanding different concepts without much effort. Their critical thinking benefits from the stories they are confronted with. Generally, it can be said that they learn how to think independently instead of being constantly spoon-fed.

The equation is an easy one: The more children read, the better they become at reading. The more interesting and enjoyable the texts they read are, the more they will want to read in general. Furthermore, by reading children automatically build their vocabulary and improve their command of language as well as of their communication skills. By reading children are exposed to a great variety of grammatical structures and phrases. In addition, being good at reading has an immediate effect on their spoken and written language skills.

What people have to begin to understand is that reading does not have to be considered annoying or tiresome. Pick the right book or text and you will experience quite the opposite! Reading enriches people's lives because it allows them to lose themselves in different worlds – their own worlds of imagination – and to gain knowledge of everything one can possibly think about.

It is the ability to evaluate, process and question the world we live in that makes us stand out from the rest. By giving up reading we give up an important part of our independence!

Prime Time 5. Testen und Fördern, Arbeitsheft (ISBN 978-3-209-08441-5)

1. What is meant by "imposition" in the second paragraph?

- ☐ an activity
- ☐ a benefit
- ☐ a hardship

2. Who likes spending their time with things other than reading?

- ☐ children and teenagers
- ☐ children and adults
- ☐ children, teenagers and adults

3. "People who understand the importance of reading keep pointing out how crucial it is that we do not stop reading but that we learn to appreciate the benefit of it." What does "it" at the end of the sentence refer to?

- ☐ importance
- ☐ reading
- ☐ benefit

4. When should children be made familiar with books?

- ☐ before they can read
- ☐ as soon as they can read
- ☐ when they understand the books

5. What makes people like reading?

- ☐ They improve their grammatical knowledge.
- ☐ They develop their communication skills.
- ☐ They are interested in the stories.

Prime Time 5. Testen und Fördern, Arbeitsheft (ISBN 978-3-209-08441-5)

4. Reading: About the guilt felt after shopping

You are going to read a text about the guilt many women feel after shopping. For statements 1-6, choose the answer (True or False) which fits best according to what you read.

About the guilt felt after shopping

According to a recent study, women spend about eight years of their lives shopping. The study was initiated by GE Money and included 3.000 female subjects. Over an estimated period of 63 years, the average woman spends approximately 25.000 hours shopping for food and clothes for both their families and themselves.

The study revealed that a woman makes about 300 shopping trips a year, lasting approximately 340 hours altogether. Considering that shopping for food just to refill the refrigerator and stock the pantry can last up to an hour if the shopping list is long, women spend more than 90 hours in supermarkets every year.

In one year, 90 trips are made to keep their closet up to date. While women go shopping for clothes about 30 times, they go shopping for shoes 15 times, for toiletries 27 times and for accessories 18 times. Buying gifts for friends and family takes up 36 hours every year.

Women do not only go shopping when it is necessary, however. More and more women use shopping to cope with everyday obstacles, emotional problems or stress. Retail therapy is not a myth or something to crack jokes about. There is scientific proof that women, and a growing number of men too, take comfort in spending money when feeling down. The drawback of uncontrolled and unnecessary shopping sprees is that most women feel bad after them.

Women are usually excited and experience joy and satisfaction while shopping. As soon as they are home, looking at all the things they have bought without really needing them and thinking about the amount of money they have spent, a sense of guilt grows inside of them. For those who have to explain their expenses to their partners it might even be worse.

Looking at the numbers, it can be said that eight out of ten women feel bad after a shopping spree. The good mood is quickly followed by guilt and shame. Three quarters of women even start feeling like this while they are still in the shop. Interestingly enough, the guilt felt shortly afterwards does not keep women from continuing their shopping trip. They rather accept that they will have to deal with their negative feelings at a later time.

In today's society it is, however, not easy to resist all those glamorous and tempting things one can buy. Wherever we look we are told that by consuming something we will either look great or feel good. But as long as we do not develop a habit of compulsive shopping, which is actually considered an addiction, going on a shopping spree once in a while should not be a problem.

Prime Time 5. Testen und Fördern, Arbeitsheft (ISBN 978-3-209-08441-5)

1. The study looked at any kind of shopping.

☐ True

☐ False

2. Food shopping usually takes an hour.

☐ True

☐ False

3. A lot of women are in therapy to overcome their shopping habits.

☐ True

☐ False

4. Guilt about shopping grows when other people are involved.

☐ True

☐ False

5. The need to go shopping is stronger than the feelings of guilt.

☐ True

☐ False

6. Compulsive shopping is considered a less serious addiction.

☐ True

☐ False

Prime Time 5. Testen und Fördern, Arbeitsheft (ISBN 978-3-209-08441-5)

5. Language in use: Fudge

You are going to read a text about how to make fudge. In most lines of the text there is an unnecessary word. Write the unnecessary word in the space provided after each line. Some lines are correct. Indicate these with a tick (✓).

Fudge is a sort of confectionery often flavored up with cocoa, which is	___________
famous for its sweetness and richness. When making fudge you have to mix with the	___________
following ingredients: milk, butter and sugar. The mixture is then heated on at 116°C,	___________
which is also called the 'soft-ball' stage. While cooling, you have to beat it, so that it	___________
will becomes a smooth and creamy substance. If you would like to make chocolate	___________
fudge, just add together chocolate to the mixture. Of course, you can also	___________
experiment with all sorts of ingredients and from flavors.	___________
One of the most more important things about making fudge is getting its texture right.	___________
Heating it at the correct temperature is what is necessary for that. It is actually the	___________
temperature that can distinguishes hard caramel from fudge. The higher the top	___________
temperature, the more sugar is dissolved and the more water disappears.	___________

6. Language in use: Extraterrestrial life

Complete the text with the words from the list. There are two extra words that you should not use.

belonging	**blessed**	**comes**	**existing**	**going**	**have**
include	**know**	**prove**	**refer**	**search**	**talk**

The word "extraterrestrial" ___________ from the Latin words "extra", which means "not of", and "terrestris", which is "___________ to earth". Everything that does not ___________ its roots on earth is therefore considered extraterrestrial life.

The various forms of extraterrestrial life ___________ bacteria-like organisms as well as human-like beings that are thought to be more sophisticated and advanced than we are. So far we are not in the position to ___________ whether such forms of life exist. Scientists, for example, ___________ for evidence of unicellular life ___________ within the Solar System. Regular people most commonly ___________ about aliens and the appearance of UFOs when they ___________ to extraterrestrial life. There are, in fact, a lot of people who believe that the Earth can, by no means, be the only planet ___________ with life.

Prime Time 5. Testen und Fördern, Arbeitsheft (ISBN 978-3-209-08441-5)

7. Writing: Now and Then (Letter)

Your English teacher has started a new project called „Now and Then“. Among other things, every student has to write a letter of about 190 words about a very emotional childhood memory. Write about one situation in which you felt extremely happy.

Make sure to include the following points:

- your age
- the situation you were in
- the people involved
- your feelings

Prime Time 5. Testen und Fördern, Arbeitsheft (ISBN 978-3-209-08441-5)

Fertigkeit	Aufgabe in Testen und Fördern	Entsprechung in Schülerbuch Prime Time 5	Seite
Listening	*The Maitreya Project (MC)*	**3** In the news. You are going to listen to a news story about Tibet. (**short answers**) **2** Just you wait! Listen to the dialogue and fill in the missing words. (**gap-filling**)	89 120f.
Listening	*Mice (T/F)*	**1+2** Tolerance and respect. (1. Who should respect whom? 2. Think before you talk) (**questions + open**) **2** Two job interviews. (**taking notes**)	93 124
Reading	*The Importance of Reading (MC)*	**2** The language school. Read the text below about a language school in the UK. Parts of the text have been removed. (**multiple matching**) **1** Heroes: The power of pictures. (**questions**)	12 95
Reading	*About the Guilt Felt after Shopping (T/F)*	**1** Job descriptions. (**questions**) **3+4** A book review of Holes by Louis Sacher. (**multiple matching + questions**)	120 129

Prime Time 5. Testen und Fördern, Arbeitsheft (ISBN 978-3-209-08441-5)

Fertigkeit	Aufgabe in Testen und Fördern	Entsprechung in Schülerbuch Prime Time 5	Seite
LiU	*Fudge (editing)*	**1+2** Passive constructions. (**open**)	11
LiU	*Extraterrestrial Life (gap-filling)*	**3** The Civil Rights Movement. You are going to read a text about the civil rights movement in the USA. Some words of the text are missing. (**gap-filling**) **3** Word formation. You are going to read a text about the painter Vincent van Gogh. Some words are missing from the text. (**word formation**)	97 85

Prime Time 5. Testen und Fördern, Arbeitsheft (ISBN 978-3-209-08441-5)

1. Listening: A casual conversation

You will hear part of a conversation between Angela and Sharon. For questions 1–5, choose the answer which fits best according to what you hear.

1. Where are the two women?

☐ in a restaurant

☐ in a bar

☐ in a café

2. Who are the two people talking?

☐ students at high school

☐ interns at a hospital

☐ freshmen at university

3. What is Angela studying?

☐ Information Technology

☐ foreign languages

☐ medicine

Prime Time 5. Testen und Fördern, Arbeitsheft (ISBN 978-3-209-08441-5)

4. Why is the exam mentioned a tough one?

- ☐ Because it is an oral exam.
- ☐ Because the workload is high.
- ☐ Because the instructor is a problem.

5. What did Sharon NOT do at the hospital?

- ☐ She took a patient's blood sample.
- ☐ She signed a prescription.
- ☐ She put a cast on a patient's leg.

Prime Time 5. Testen und Fördern, Arbeitsheft (ISBN 978-3-209-08441-5)

2. Listening: Music as a means of stress relief

You will hear part of a radio report about how music can help people deal with stress. For statements 1–7, choose the answer (True or False) which fits best according to what you hear.

1. Every form of music can be considered art.

☐ True

☐ False

2. Only people with a certain cultural knowledge enjoy music.

☐ True

☐ False

3. Classical music in particular helps you overcome stress.

☐ True

☐ False

Prime Time 5. Testen und Fördern, Arbeitsheft (ISBN 978-3-209-08441-5)

4. Music can completely replace your social contacts.

☐ True

☐ False

5. The melody is as important as the story behind a song.

☐ True

☐ False

6. While listening to music to relax, you should not be disturbed.

☐ True

☐ False

7. This report informs the listeners about the healing power of music.

☐ True

☐ False

Prime Time 5. Testen und Fördern, Arbeitsheft (ISBN 978-3-209-08441-5)

3. Reading: Getting about in Greater Bristol

You are going to read a text on a website called *Getting About in Greater Bristol*. For statements 1–6, choose the answer (True, False or Not Given) which fits best according to what you read.

Getting About in Greater Bristol

Getting About in Greater Bristol is a website which provides all sorts of travel information for disabled people wanting to go to Greater Bristol, the area containing and surrounding the city of Bristol in the South West of England. This site has got information on transport for Bath and North East Somerset, Bristol, North Somerset as well as South Gloucestershire.

Due to the influence the Disability Discrimination Act has had on transport, both public transport and places in the Greater Bristol area are constantly being made more accessible.

Since some changes can only be brought about gradually, our website has the aim to help less mobile or disabled people to find their way around the area more easily. It includes recent changes and improvements in access to trains, buses, taxis, community transport services, bus stations, train stations as well as airports. We put a lot of effort in being up to date at all times.

This website introduces people to how to get about in the area using different means of transport and at the same time provides detailed information on transportation that disabled people look for when planning their journeys. Direct links to other sources than transportation and travel websites will make your travel planning even easier.

Finding accommodation suitable for disabled people plays an essential role when making travel arrangements. *Tourism for All* is a national charity and the UK Voice for Accessible Tourism. *Tourism for All* has managed to build up a remarkably good reputation because they have overcome various obstacles or difficulties people with disabilities or older people face when going on a trip. You will find a link to their homepage on our website.

Another link we provide is *Visit Britain*. Regardless of whether you need some practical travel advice or specific information on health insurances or visas, *Visit Britain* can answer your questions. Among other things, it also includes information on British culture.

We are proud to say that England and the Greater Bristol area in particular extend a very warm welcome to disabled visitors and their carers. A lot of public places, including tourist attractions of all sorts, have already been made accessible to people using wheelchairs. Restaurants and hotels have taken all the necessary precautions too.
We will, of course, keep investing our energy and resources in improving our environment for people with disabilities.

Prime Time 5. Testen und Fördern, Arbeitsheft (ISBN 978-3-209-08441-5)

1. *Getting About in Greater Bristol* is a website dedicated to all kinds of tourists.

- ☐ True
- ☐ False
- ☐ Not Given

2. Greater Bristol is known for its modern technology in public transport.

- ☐ True
- ☐ False
- ☐ Not Given

3. In Greater Bristol, public transport and places could not be made more accessible.

- ☐ True
- ☐ False
- ☐ Not Given

4. The website tries to post new developments immediately.

- ☐ True
- ☐ False
- ☐ Not Given

Prime Time 5. Testen und Fördern, Arbeitsheft (ISBN 978-3-209-08441-5)

5. The website also refers people to other transportation websites.

- ☐ True
- ☐ False
- ☐ Not Given

6. This text points out a speciality in tourism in the Greater Bristol area.

- ☐ True
- ☐ False
- ☐ Not Given

Prime Time 5. Testen und Fördern, Arbeitsheft (ISBN 978-3-209-08441-5)

4. Reading: Excessive use of media in teenagers

You are going to read a text on excessive use of media in teenagers. For questions 1–5, choose the answer which fits best according to what you read.

Excessive use of media in teenagers

Children and teenagers say that they are in full control of the amount of time they spend using all sorts of media and that they would be able to stop media consumption at any time. However, more and more young people are overwhelmed with the great variety of media-related input they are confronted with every day. They frequently do not even realize any more how many hours they spend playing video games, chatting with their friends on the phone, updating their profiles on social networking sites or just watching TV.

A lot of parents get the impression that their children are addicted to media consumption, which is an alarming fact. In the past few years, it has been observed that media replace essential activities in young people's lives, ranging from the replacement of physical activity and homework to the replacement of important personal relationships. If this is the case, parents need to set up easy and clear rules and try to change their children's behavior.

Media and the body

Most of the media young people consume ask for sitting. They either sit in front of the TV on the couch or in front of their computer screen on a chair or they might even lie in bed sending text messages to their friends while having their notebooks sitting on their laps. Either way, young people are generally more sedentary when consuming media, except for those listening to their iPods while jogging or doing their workout on an exercise bike.

What is even worse than just sitting is the fact that most young people take in a lot of unhealthy food while sitting. Consuming junk food frequently goes hand in hand with consuming media. If there is no exercise whatsoever, the circumstances mentioned above can quickly lead to weight gain and other physical problems.

Media and homework

Many young people are so extremely absorbed in whatever kind of media they are using that they do not feel time passing. It is the entertainment and excitement they experience when playing games or communicating with peers via the phone or Internet that makes them forget everything else, their homework included. While this may have an immediate negative effect on their marks, they also miss out on a lot of personal development and growth.

Prime Time 5. Testen und Fördern, Arbeitsheft (ISBN 978-3-209-08441-5)

Media and relationships

The effects excessive media consumption can have are twofold. On the one hand, it can lead to complete isolation. Young people might turn away from family and friends because there is no time for personal interaction due to the time spent making one's way to all the levels in a video game, for example. On the other hand, there might be over-communication. Today, people can play video games online together with other people. They are communicating with each other all the time, but unfortunately not in person. While this certainly is some sort of interaction, it is not one that promotes the development of good social skills.

If parents have children who fit that pattern, they need to take the situation at home seriously and do something about it. As a first step, parents and children need to sit down together and discuss possible changes in the children's media usage habits. Setting up strict rules that do not make much sense, like forbidding media consumption altogether, is the wrong thing to do. Instead, parents should build on the suggestions their children have and work out a good and fair set of rules together.

1. What does 'are overwhelmed with' in the first paragraph mean?

- ☐ to be in control of
- ☐ to be flooded with
- ☐ to be excited about

2. How do teenagers compensate for their lack of exercise when consuming media?

- ☐ They consume a lot of healthy food.
- ☐ They do a lot of sports.
- ☐ They often do not compensate for it.

Prime Time 5. Testen und Fördern, Arbeitsheft (ISBN 978-3-209-08441-5)

3. Why do teenagers frequently not do their homework?

- ☐ They are not interested in doing it.
- ☐ They do not have enough time for it.
- ☐ They do not think it affects their marks.

4. How does the writer of the text see online communication?

- ☐ It is a good way to communicate with more people at the same time.
- ☐ In combination with real-life, people are communicating too much.
- ☐ It has a negative influence on people's communication skills.

5. How should parents react to excessive media usage?

- ☐ They should take their children's opinions seriously.
- ☐ They should change their own media usage habits.
- ☐ They should present their children with strict rules.

Prime Time 5. Testen und Fördern, Arbeitsheft (ISBN 978-3-209-08441-5)

5. Language in use: Google

You are going to read a text about Google. In most lines of the text there is an unnecessary word. Write the unnecessary word in the space provided after each line. Some lines are correct. Indicate these with a tick (✓).

Google is an American multinational public corporation. It also operates in the fields ____________
of Internet search, from advertising technologies and cloud computing, which is ____________
Internet-based computing. ____________
Sergey Brin and Larry Page, who also known as the 'Google Guys', founded the ____________
company in 1998. Its initial public offering took place in 2004. Their headquarters ____________
are in around Mountain View, California, where they have been since 2006. The ____________
company's mission statement has always been to make all the information available ____________
in the world to accessible to everybody. ____________
While the company's core is its web and search engine, Google now offers a wide ____________
variety of applications and from tools, ranging from online productivity software like ____________
Gmail and social networking tools like Google Buzz to the web browser Google ____________
Chrome or as the service Google Books. ____________
Google Search, Google's web search engine, is still being the company's most popular ____________
service. In the United States alone, Google is the dominant search engine only, ____________
holding a market share of approximately 66%. ____________

Prime Time 5. Testen und Fördern, Arbeitsheft (ISBN 978-3-209-08441-5)

6. Language in use: Stand-up comedy

Read the text on stand-up comedy. Some words are missing. Use the words in brackets to form words that fit in the gaps. Write your answers in the gaps.

Stand-up comedy is a particular kind of comedy in which the comedian is on stage, performing in front of a live audience, (1) .... (**general**) speaking directly to them and (2) .... (**involve**) them in his act. High-profile comedians are often filmed during their (3) .... (**perform**) so that their shows can be made available via DVD, television or the Internet.

The person standing on stage is (4) .... (**refer**) to as "stand-up comedian", "comic" or just "stand-up".

Stand-up performances are generally fairly short and are (5) .... (**characterise**) by short jokes, one-liners and (6) .... (**humour**) stories which are presented one after the other without much (7) .... (**interrupt**).
There are stand-ups who use music or magic tricks to spice up their performances. The performances themselves usually take place in comedy clubs and bars or colleges and theatres.

Being (8) .... (**success**) as a stand-up comedian is the result of hard work.
Very often comedians work (9) .... (**incredible**) long for very short programmes, which they keep improving while repeatedly performing them on stage.

Prime Time 5. Testen und Fördern, Arbeitsheft (ISBN 978-3-209-08441-5)

7. Writing: Reality TV shows (Short text)

Together with a group of friends you have watched a reality TV show. State your opinion towards shows like "Big Brother", "The Real World" or "The Osbournes" in about 190 words.

Make sure to include the following points:

- what is typical for reality TV shows
- how often you watch them
- why you watch or do not watch them
- whether you would take part in one

Prime Time 5. Testen und Fördern, Arbeitsheft (ISBN 978-3-209-08441-5)

Fertigkeit	Aufgabe in Testen und Fördern	Entsprechung in Schülerbuch Prime Time 5	Seite
Listening	*A Casual Conversation (MC)*	**2** Not the only show in town. You are going to listen to an interview with a language expert. (**short answers**)	9
		9 Just another pizza order in Manhattan. A New York City radio station recorded a strange dialogue for its "Believe or not" show. Manhattan banker Dale Dupont called in with his story. (**short answers**)	10
		4 Walkabout. You are going to listen to two students talking about Walkabout on the phone. (**multiple matching**)	33
Listening	*Music as a Means of Stress Relief (T/F)*	**2** Docusoaps. Read the text below about the TV genre "docusoap". Parts of the text have been removed. Choose the correct part for the gaps. (**multiple matching**)	49f.
		6 Charlie's video blog. You are going to listen to a conversation about Charlie's internet activities. (**short answers**)	102
Reading	*Getting about in Greater Bristol (T/F/NG)*	**3** UK 2005 election statistics. Read the text below, then decide whether the statements are true or false. (**T/F**)	72f.
		4 Publishing one's own writing. (**short answers**)	132

Prime Time 5. Testen und Fördern, Arbeitsheft (ISBN 978-3-209-08441-5)

Fertigkeit	Aufgabe in Testen und Fördern	Entsprechung in Schülerbuch Prime Time 5	Seite
Reading	*Excessive Use of Media in Teenagers (MC)*	**1–3** Facebook **1** Read the following article about social networking sites and add headlines on the dotted lines for each paragraph. **2** Understanding the text. Select the option that reflects the information in the text most accurately. (**MC 1 aus 3**) **3** Questions (Facebook)	24 24 25
LiU	*Google (editing)*	**4** Participles or infinitives after verbs of perception. (**gap-filling**) **3** Conditional 3: Talking about imaginary situations in the past. (**matching + open**)	125 135
LiU	*Stand-Up Comedy (word formation)*	**4** Union in danger. You are going to read a text about Scottish independence. Some words are missing from the text. Choose the correct answer for each gap. (**MC gap-filling**)	73

Prime Time 5. Testen und Fördern, Arbeitsheft (ISBN 978-3-209-08441-5)

1. Listening: Facebook

You will hear a discussion between two students about Facebook. For statements 1–6, choose the answer (True or False) which fits best according to what you hear.

1. This is the second discussion taking place this week.

☐ True

☐ False

2. Today millions of users must use Facebook.

☐ True

☐ False

3. Simon thinks Facebook is the best social platform.

☐ True

☐ False

Prime Time 5. Testen und Fördern, Arbeitsheft (ISBN 978-3-209-08441-5)

4. Lisa is not against online communication.

☐ True

☐ False

5. Simon argues that the owners of Facebook are not allowed to keep personal information.

☐ True

☐ False

6. Many people use Facebook to avoid going out.

☐ True

☐ False

Prime Time 5. Testen und Fördern, Arbeitsheft (ISBN 978-3-209-08441-5)

2. Listening: Greek-Americans

You will hear part of a radio report about Greek-Americans. For questions 1–5, choose the answer which fits best according to what you hear.

1. Which of the following is the main religion in Greece?

- ☐ the Roman Catholic Church
- ☐ the Eastern Orthodox Church
- ☐ the Greek Catholic Church

2. When did the first Greek arrive in America?

- ☐ in the 16th century
- ☐ in the 18th century
- ☐ in the 19th century

3. Why did many Greeks leave their home country?

- ☐ because of religious persecution
- ☐ because of poor living conditions
- ☐ because of the economy

Prime Time 5. Testen und Fördern, Arbeitsheft (ISBN 978-3-209-08441-5)

4. What kind of business did most Greeks in Tarpon Springs work in?

☐ sponge selling

☐ sponge diving

☐ sponge manufacturing

5. What is the purpose of this report?

☐ to inform the listeners about the Greek-Americans' lifestyle

☐ to criticize the Greek-Americans' way of living

☐ to persuade the listeners to visit Tarpon Springs

Prime Time 5. Testen und Fördern, Arbeitsheft (ISBN 978-3-209-08441-5)

3. Reading: The trouble with boys in school

You are going to read a text on the trouble with boys in school. For questions 1–5, choose the answer which fits best according to what you read.

The trouble with boys in school

This is to comment on the lecture my classmates and I listened to at school today. Peg Tyre, an acclaimed American journalist and writer, presented her book 'The Trouble With Boys' in our assembly hall today.

She started out by telling us about a 16-year-old boy who seems to be a very bright, thoughtful and nice teenager when talking to him outside of school. His relationship with his parents is a very good one. He likes rock music and plays the guitar regularly. However, as soon as he enters his school building in Salt Lake City he gets extremely nervous and puts on a fearful look. In class, he quickly loses focus and therefore often misses important information. His teachers do not have the time to explain things twice because they have to deal with approximately 36 students per class, and he has already been classified as stupid and lazy even though he can perform excellently when not put under pressure.

According to Peg Tyre, this boy's description fits a lot of young boys today. Statistics say that more and more boys are falling behind in our school system. In elementary school, for example, boys are two times more likely to be diagnosed with learning disabilities than girls. In higher classes, the problems continue with boys falling behind with regard to standardized writing tests, just to mention one aspect. Statistics also show that the number of boys disliking school has risen about 71% in the past 30 years. As far as the future is concerned, Tyre does not believe that the gap between boys and girls will close soon.

I can only confirm that boys tend to get lower grades than girls. The reasons for this vary, of course. One might be that both students and teachers act under a lot of pressure nowadays. There are states in the US in which teachers do not really have a say in when and how they will teach their students certain things. Quite on the contrary, teachers are told by the state what, when and how to teach, leaving the students' abilities totally out of consideration. The standardized tests students have to take do not allow for a lot of time to process the materials students are presented with every single day. It is basically about memorizing one fact after the other, without ever asking what they think about these facts.

Another reason I believe to be responsible for the boys' lower achievement is that in many cases boys are asked to behave like girls. They are told to sit still, focus and just be quiet. There is not much room for running around, screaming or just letting off some steam. Sports classes have even been cut in favor of more theory-based subjects.

One more thing that I consider important is that more and more boys do not like reading. The media we have access to make it easy to find something other to do than read. While girls seem to like reading, boys often think of it as something unmanly, which, of course, is not true. I prefer ending my day with a book, but my friends do not necessarily know that because they would rather play soccer or hit the town.

To sum it up, I have to say that I enjoyed listening to Peg Tyre. The statistics and stories she presented were very interesting and shocking at the same time. I hope that politicians, educators, teachers and parents will soon figure out a way to put the boys in this country back on track because they deserve a fair chance in life.

Prime Time 5. Testen und Fördern, Arbeitsheft (ISBN 978-3-209-08441-5)

1. Why did Peg Tyre start her lecture with the example of a 16-year-old boy?

- ☐ to illustrate why teachers do not have time to repeat information
- ☐ to illustrate in what ways teenage boys react to school
- ☐ to illustrate the influence of the parents on teenage boys

2. Why do boys fall behind at school?

- ☐ Because the structure of writing tests has changed.
- ☐ Because they are not interested in school.
- ☐ Because they have difficulties studying.

3. What does the writer criticize about the school system?

- ☐ The states have too much influence on the information presented.
- ☐ The teachers do not care about what the students are interested in.
- ☐ The students are presented with too much detailed information.

4. What is the writer's attitude towards reading?

- ☐ He knows reading is important but thinks only girls should do it.
- ☐ He sometimes reads but prefers doing sports or going out.
- ☐ He likes reading but tries to hide it from his friends.

5. What sort of text is this?

- ☐ personal statement
- ☐ descriptive essay
- ☐ formal letter

Prime Time 5. Testen und Fördern, Arbeitsheft (ISBN 978-3-209-08441-5)

4. Reading: Meg comes to see me in Aussie Land!

You are going to read a blog entry written by Karen, who is currently in Australia. For statements 1–7, choose the answer (True or False) which fits best according to what you read.

This goes to my dearest friends and all my faithful readers! I hereby sincerely apologize for not posting anything in the last two weeks, which is usually so not me but I simply couldn't find the time to do so because … Can you believe it?! My best friend Meg came to see me in the land of Aussies and stayed for almost twelve days! The time we spent together was so exciting and packed with fun, laughter, and unforgettable experiences! I hope you can forgive me ☺
Ok, back to the story!
Meg arrived in Brisbane on July 3. I was so excited about her arrival even days before I actually saw her again after – what seemed to me like – an eternity!
On her arrival day we did nothing but have coffee and talk about everything that was new with her.
The first three days we only spent around Brisbane. I was busy showing her the ins and outs of this great city while she was trying to keep up with soaking in all the beauty this place has to offer. We even got round to meeting my new friends on campus. They seemed to like each other, which I find cool.
Apart from eating the most delicious food in some of the smaller restaurants and bars in Brisbane and doing excessive shopping once or twice, we just had the best time doing nothing but laughing our heads off.
On Meg's fourth day in Australia we went to Cairns, which is very close to the Great Barrier Reef, a fantastic place for scuba diving, snorkeling and reef cruising. After having a very tasty breakfast in a cute little café, we decided to lie out in the grass a little since you won't find beaches in Cairns. I swear … we only lay there for an hour! You wouldn't believe what 1 hour of Aussie sun can do to your body. Looking in the mirror back in the hotel we couldn't believe our eyes: We were roasted!!! Meg started to laugh hysterically and called me a lobster! ☺
The next day we were headed to the Great Barrier Reef. Meg desperately wanted to go there, which was fine by me since I love the GBR.
While snorkeling on various reefs we saw so many different kinds of coral and fish. You wouldn't believe the variety of beautiful and colorful fish you get so see there. What's even better is the water! It's crystal clear!!! Just like in the movies!
Time flew when Meg was with me. If I wrote down everything that we did, it would probably take me hours, which I don't have because class starts in about 50 minutes.
There is just one more thing we did that I would like to share with you because it was great fun. One day we went to Steve Irwin Australia Zoo, north of Brisbane. I had wanted to go there all semester and I figured it was even better to go there with my best friend. We got to play with some kangaroos and koalas. The little koala babies in the animal hospital were the cutest thing in the world I have ever seen. We felt like cuddling them and taking them home with us. Our zoo day was just an awesome day!
Oh, it's late. I have to run …
You all know that I am having a great time here in Brissy but I also miss my family and friends a lot. It's only another four weeks and I will get to go back home! Can't wait to see you all again!
Love, Karen

Prime Time 5. Testen und Fördern, Arbeitsheft (ISBN 978-3-209-08441-5)

1. Karen cares about updating her friends at home.

☐ True

☐ False

2. On Meg's first day in Brisbane the girls talked about what had been going on in both their lives.

☐ True

☐ False

3. Karen is glad Meg and her Aussie friends got along well.

☐ True

☐ False

4. The first days were full of exciting trips.

☐ True

☐ False

5. The girls got sunburned while snorkeling the Great Barrier Reef.

☐ True

☐ False

6. Karen has tried to include everything in her blog that she and Meg did.

☐ True

☐ False

7. Karen will leave Brisbane in not more than four weeks.

☐ True

☐ False

Prime Time 5. Testen und Fördern, Arbeitsheft (ISBN 978-3-209-08441-5)

5. Language in use: Airplanes and environmental concerns

Read through the text and choose the correct answer (A or B) for each gap (1–9) in the text.

One of the consequences of global economic growth is the (1) ….. increase in air travel. While airlines are (2) ….. satisfied with the steadily growing numbers of passengers taking to the skies and the transportation taken care of via airplanes, there are at the same time more and more (3) ….. concerns.

Airplane emissions have been identified as (4) ….. contributing to the greenhouse effect and therefore to climate change. Experts expect a (5) ….. 50% rise in carbon dioxide emissions by the middle of the 21st century. Compared to cars, the (6) ….. emissions coming from airplanes contribute to climate change three times as much because planes emit their gases (7) ….. in the atmosphere.

(8) ….., the Kyoto Protocol, an international agreement on climate change, does not set any restrictions on carbon dioxide emissions caused by air travel, although planes are (9) ….. for emitting 600 million tons of CO_2 every year.

(1) A constant B constantly
(2) A incredible B incredibly
(3) A environmental B environmentally
(4) A critical B critically
(5) A dramatic B dramatically
(6) A enormous B enormously
(7) A high B highly
(8) A interesting B interestingly
(9) A responsible B responsibly

Prime Time 5. Testen und Fördern, Arbeitsheft (ISBN 978-3-209-08441-5)

6. Language in use: Eating healthy food

Complete the text with the words from the list. There are two extra words that you should not use.

are – are made – comes – cutting – do – do not – is – need – think – will realize

When it (1) .... to eating healthy food, a lot of people (2) .... that this means eating food that does not taste good or look nice. What they immediately think about are Brussels sprouts, cauliflower, goat cheese or tofu, when in fact healthy food (3) .... much more than that. It is basically about eating enough fruits, vegetables, oily fish and whole grain foods while (4) .... back on things like red meat, sugary drinks and refined grains.

A healthy diet is about keeping the balance. If you (5) .... willing to experiment a little, you (6) .... how exciting, tasty and exotic other kinds of food can be.

There is one myth you should bear in mind! Vegetarian dishes are not always healthier than non-vegetarian dishes. There are quite a few vegetarian dishes that (7) .... with lots of oil, sauces and cheese. They are also often fried, which is why they (8) .... always qualify as healthy dishes.

Prime Time 5. Testen und Fördern, Arbeitsheft (ISBN 978-3-209-08441-5)

7. Writing: The upset passenger (E-mail)

You were on the bus home from school today, talking and texting to your friends on your cell phone. Another passenger got angry because of all the noise, and screamed at you.

You are at home now but still totally upset about that and decide to share your experience with your friends via email.

Make sure to include the following points:

- short description of your phone activities
- the passenger's behavior
- your reaction
- how you felt afterwards

Write your email in 170–200 words.

Prime Time 5. Testen und Fördern, Arbeitsheft (ISBN 978-3-209-08441-5)

Förderhinweise

Fertigkeit	Aufgabe in Testen und Fördern	Entsprechung in Schülerbuch Prime Time 5	Seite
Listening	*Facebook (T/F)*	**1** Interviews about the use of media. You are going to listen to two interviews with teenagers about their use of the media. (**T/F**)	58
		1 Reality shows. You are going to listen to a family discussion about reality shows. (**MC 1 aus 4**)	82
Listening	*Greek-Americans (MC)*	**1** How American democracy began. (**MC 1 aus 4**)	69
		2 Marco's, Pete's and Naomi's work experience. You are going to listen to what students Marco, Pete and Naomi say about the work experience they did in Year 10. (**multiple matching**)	116
Reading	*The trouble with Boys in School (MC)*	**2–5** Deportation at breakfast. (**questions**)	79f.
		1+2 Dignity for all? The concept of dignity. (**open + questions**)	88f.
Reading	*Meg comes to see me in Aussie Land (T/F)*	**1+2** Walkabout. Reasons to be afraid? Read the following extract from an Australian novel. (**questions**)	32f.
		1+2 Angela. Why did I have to say that?! Read the following extract from the novel by Angela by James Moloney. (**questions**)	34f.

Prime Time 5. Testen und Fördern, Arbeitsheft (ISBN 978-3-209-08441-5)

Fertigkeit	Aufgabe in Testen und Fördern	Entsprechung in Schülerbuch Prime Time 5	Seite
LiU	*Airplanes and Environmental Concerns (adjective-adverb gap-filling)*	**1** Forms of comparison. Fill in the forms of comparison in the following sentences. Choose the correct phrases. (**gap-filling**)	66
		3 Choose the correct form (adjective or adverb) (**open**)	111
LiU	*Eating Healthy Food (tenses – gap-filling)*	**3** Lucy's interview. Complete the dialogue with the correct future forms). (**gap-filling**)	19
		3 Past or present perfect forms? Complete the dialogue with the correct past forms or present perfect forms. (**gap-filling**)	26
		4 Present and past tenses. Complete the dialogue with the correct tenses. (**gap-filling**)	29

Prime Time 5. Testen und Fördern, Arbeitsheft (ISBN 978-3-209-08441-5)

1. Listening: Actionwork

You will hear part of a radio programme in which Brian Williams interviews Roanna Burton about 'Actionwork'. For questions 1–5, choose the answer which fits best according to what you hear.

1. What audience does TOLF address?

- ☐ adults in their 30s
- ☑ **teenagers**
- ☐ elderly people

2. What media does 'Actionwork' use to promote its ideas?

- ☐ print media
- ☐ radio and the Internet
- ☑ **movies and plays**

3. Since when has 'Actionwork' been active?

- ☐ since 1919
- ☐ since 2003
- ☑ **since 1990**

4. 'Actionwork' deals with a lot of different problems. Which of these problems is NOT mentioned in the interview?

- ☑ **cyber bullying**
- ☐ peer pressure
- ☐ illegal substances

5. In how far my bullying change the victims' character?

- ☐ They may turn aggressive later in life.
- ☐ They may become self-centered and selfish people.
- ☑ **They may be frightened and stop trusting themselves.**

Prime Time 5. Testen und Fördern, Arbeitsheft (ISBN 978-3-209-08441-5)

Tapescript: Actionwork

RA	Welcome to TOLF, your radio station for today's younger generation. Hey, I am Brian Williams and this is "Top Story of the Week". With me today is Roanna Burton, a member of the 'Actionwork' staff, a Theatre and Film in Education company. They are in the middle of planning their 8th National Anti-Bullying Conference in the UK, taking place in November … Hi Roanna, welcome to TOLF, I'm glad you're with us today.
RO	Hello Brian, thanks for inviting me. I'm really happy to be here too.
RA	Could you tell us what it basically is that you do at 'Actionwork'?
RO	As you already said, we are a Theatre and Film in Education company and as such try to promote empowerment and reduce bullying and violence in schools. It is high quality work that we produce in a number of different media. You could actually get very detailed information about our activities on our website if you want to.
RA	I will surely check that one out later. Em … Since when has 'Actionwork' been around?
RO	'Actionwork' was founded in 1990 by Andy Hickson. And since then a great variety of extremely talented and committed performers, directors, choreographers, filmmakers and facilitators have been creating the best in film and theatre in education.
RA	That sounds just great! Uhm, what are … uhm … what are some of the issues that you tackle with your performances?
RO	Well, there's really quite a range of issues … uhm … that we deal with. Everything that has to do with young people … starting with bullying and racism, then … drugs, relationships, teenage pregnancy or peer pressure. It's basically everything and anything that affects young people's lives.
RA	… and now you are planning your 8th National Anti-Bullying Conference, taking place from the 15th to the 19th of November.
RO	Yes, and we are already really excited about that! Since we first started with this conference in 2003, we have been attracting more and more people with our event. They are coming from everywhere, even from abroad. It's become a huge thing and we are really proud of it. It clearly shows us that more and more people are becoming aware of the different kinds of bullying that are out there, harming people … destroying lives.
RA	"We are giving young people a voice" is what I read in your latest brochure about your very special and still unique annual conference.
RO	This is actually our main aim! We are reaching out to both, victims and perpetrators, those who suffer and those who make others suffer. We want them to share their story with us and by doing so, give them the opportunity to reflect upon their experiences and actions.
RA	So, you are saying you also care about the bullies?
RO	Well, there is always a reason why people bully others. I mean, even though there is no excuse for it, there is ALWAYS a reason, and we need to work with the bullies too.

RA	What could that be, for example?
RO	It's basically about the bullies feeling strong and powerful. Something has happened in their life that makes them search for the feeling of unlimited power because otherwise they feel inferior and unimportant. Very often it's negative experiences they have had at home or at school.
RA	But we must not forget about the victims either!
RO	Of course not!!! It's them who often end up incredibly unhappy, insecure and even depressed. Victims of bullying are frequently filled with fear … too afraid to leave the house … not capable of going to school or work. And what's even worse is that such people develop very low self-esteem. They often think they deserve all the bullying, which is, of course, absolutely wrong.
RA	Thank you, Roanna! This has been very informative and exciting so far.
RO	You are very welcome!
RA	'Actionwork' – The world's leading theatre and film company dealing with bullying and violence! More on that after the break … (*fade out*)

Prime Time 5. Testen und Fördern, Arbeitsheft (ISBN 978-3-209-08441-5)

Testen und Fördern

2. Listening: Mike Baker

You will hear part of a radio report in which Mike Baker talks about his career as a ski jumper. For statements 1–6, choose the correct answer (True or False) which fits best according to what you hear.

1. School kept Mike very busy.

- ☐ True
- ☑ **False**

2. Skiing fascinated him from the very beginning.

- ☑ **True**
- ☐ False

3. His uncle was a ski jumper himself.

- ☑ **True**
- ☐ False

Testen und Fördern

4. Mike had to stop ski jumping for 2 years because his family moved to another city.

- ☐ True
- ☑ **False**

5. While he attended the National Sport School, he had the chance to travel a lot.

- ☑ **True**
- ☐ False

6. He will definitely take part in the next Winter Olympics.

- ☐ True
- ☑ **False**

Prime Time 5. Testen und Fördern, Arbeitsheft (ISBN 978-3-209-08441-5)

Tapescript: Mike Baker

Hi, my name is Mike Baker. I was born in Thunder Bay, Ontario. Doing sports has been extremely important to me ever since I was a kid. In winter I usually played hockey and in summer soccer. I have to say I kept my parents pretty busy with all the extra curricular activities I was engaged in outside of school.

It wasn't until I was 11 years old, however, that I tried alpine skiing for the very first time at Mount Mackay. It was part of our 'skiing in schools' program. I was hooked from the start. Seriously, I couldn't think about anything else. I can still remember receiving my very own Dynastar skis and blue boots for Christmas. This was most definitely my favorite Christmas present of all time.

A year later my uncle offered to take me to my first ski jump. When he was younger, he was part of a semi-professional team of ski jumpers in Ottawa. Because of the stories he told me, I had always wanted to try that. December 21 was the big day. Hook, line, and sinker. Today I consider this the beginning of my life. Unfortunately, I had to quit for about two years because I was also part of a hockey team, and the two activities together took up too much time. It didn't take me long to realize that something was missing in my life, though, and after this 2-year-break I left the hockey team to join the Thunder Bay ski jumper team.

I trained really hard, spent every minute I had on the ski jump. It finally paid off when I turned 15 and was asked to join the National Ski Jumping team. Then my parents and I decided that I would attend the National Sport School in Calgary. The school was founded to support young Canadian athletes and give them the chance to train and travel both within the country and abroad, while still going to school. At the age of 18 I graduated from NSS with an Advanced Diploma.

The following years I lived through some tougher times, losing my father to a heart attack. Ski jumping was the only thing that kept me going. Even though I tried my very best, I didn't qualify for the Winter Olympic Games in Vancouver in 2010, which is okay considering that I am only 22 years old now.

My goal for the next four years is to take my profession to the next level, work with the best coaches available in my country and then be among the athletes who will be part of the next Olympic Games.

Testen und Fördern

3. Reading: How to improve your performance at school

You are going to read a text on improving your performance at school. For questions 1–5, choose the answer which fits best according to what you read.

At the beginning of a new school year many students plan on doing better at school than the year before. While they are very motivated at first, they often do not know how to get good grades in the long run. Here's a list of the most useful strategies.

Be active in all your classes. While it is very important to attend your classes regularly and pay attention to what your teachers say, it is even more important to actively participate in what is going on. Ask questions, make it known if you don't understand something, take part in class discussions, and share your experiences and opinions with your classmates and teachers.

Take good notes. Being able to take good notes is vital not only at school but also at work later on. It starts with being a good listener who is able to identify the most important information. Key points and definitions as well as diagrams should be noted down. Since you are busy during the lesson and do not have that much time to revise your notes, make sure you take a second look at them at home. Re-write them if necessary. A good structure can help you a great deal as soon as you have to study the material.

Master your teachers. You have probably noticed already that every teacher has their own style of teaching and system of grading. It is important to keep that in mind when preparing for any kind of exam and doing your homework. Make sure you know what they want and try to meet their expectations. Communicating with them is important too. Remember that they are also people who sometimes have problems understanding something. If you let them know that you are struggling, they might be able to help.

Be organized. You should not only organize your notes but also your daily schedule. Keep a diary on exam dates and homework assignments as well as presentations and papers. Plan enough time to prepare for all of them and do not try to do five different things at one time. It helps to concentrate on the more difficult things first and keep the easier ones for later. If you use your time wisely, it definitely pays off later on. You can then avoid feeling stressed and do your school work one step at a time. Still don't forget to take breaks on a regular basis.

Be a good test-taker. Your grades depend to a great extent on getting good results on exams. If you have known your teacher for a while you should know what to expect. For new teachers you could try to get copies of old tests and exams. Go to the test well-prepared …… ……. you can relax and completely focus on the tasks presented to you. Read the instructions carefully and ask any questions you might have before the test begins. It's crucial that you really understand what you have to do to perform well on the tasks. Normally you don't get the same number of points for each task, so make sure you do the ones with the highest number of points first.

Stick to our suggestions and you will improve your grades for sure! ☺

Prime Time 5. Testen und Fördern, Arbeitsheft (ISBN 978-3-209-08441-5)

1. According to the text, what is the most important thing you should do to be active in your classes?

- ☐ go to your classes regularly
- ☐ be attentive at all times
- ☐ learn how to listen
- ☑ **take part in the lesson**

2. Why should you have another look at your notes after the lesson?

- ☐ to include diagrams and definitions
- ☐ to check whether you have written down everything
- ☑ **to structure and organize your notes well**
- ☐ to write them down a second time

3. "Be organized. […] If you use your time wisely, it definitely pays off later on. […]"
What is the meaning of the phrase "to pay off" in this context?

- ☑ **You are in a better situation later on.**
- ☐ You have to do several things at a time later on.
- ☐ You are more stressed out later on.
- ☐ You have nothing to do later on.

4. "Be a good test-taker. […] Go to the test well-prepared …… …… you can relax and completely focus on the tasks presented to you."
Two words are missing in the text. Choose the words that fit best.

- ☐ because so
- ☑ **so that**
- ☐ for that
- ☐ then so

5. Who is this text written for?

- ☐ students who have problems with their teachers
- ☐ students who want to learn how to take notes
- ☑ **students who want to do well at school**
- ☐ students who have problems at home because of school

Prime Time 5. Testen und Fördern, Arbeitsheft (ISBN 978-3-209-08441-5)

4. Reading: Worlds apart

You are going to read two texts about computers and the Internet. For statements 1–8, choose the answer (True, False or Not given) which fits best according to what you read.

ATSU "Most people in my country do not have a computer of their own. For starters, it's not exactly cheap to buy and maintain one. Compared to Western countries, the ones you get here are quite expensive. I bought mine, which is a rather big one, about a year ago as a second-hand computer. Around here in Mozambique you don't get to see a lot of iPads or netbooks.

Second, access to the Internet can be problematic. I, for example, have to get up around 4 in the morning if I want to have reliable and fast service. Access happens via dial-up and as soon as there is a great number of people surfing the net at the same time, the connection slows down dramatically. Even under the best conditions I have to keep in mind my 128Kbps bandwidth.

For those who do not have Internet access at home or who cannot afford a computer in the first place, cyber cafés have become extremely popular places. Even I sometimes use them. As a journalist I depend on Internet access to be informed about what is happening around the world. Web logs in particular are very useful because they allow news to travel fast and reach lots of different people."

YON "We have seven computers at home. Two of them are mine, my husband has two as well and each of our three kids has their own. I prefer using the laptop when travelling; at home I usually work on the desktop.

Life without a computer or Internet access would be impossible for me. I have been using and working on the computer for about two decades now and I am amazed at the incredible developments in terms of size, RAM and speed at which data can be processed. Especially at work the computer comes in very handy when accessing all sorts of information and contacting people. There is no longer any need to rifle through files and I can provide my boss with up-to-date figures and numbers within minutes. At home I generally use the computer to stay in touch with family and friends. My son spends most of his time playing online games. My younger daughter uses hers for educational purposes, and our youngest loves chat rooms and social networks.

While seven computers in one household may be an exception in other countries, it's typical for a South Korean family. Here lots of people have computers and a quarter of all inhabitants use high-speed Internet."

Testen und Fördern

1. In Mozambique you cannot buy iPads or netbooks.

- ☐ True
- ☑ False
- ☐ Not given

2. To use the Internet in Mozambique you must get up at 4.

- ☐ True
- ☑ False
- ☐ Not given

3. The connection gets worse when more people are online.

- ☑ True
- ☐ False
- ☐ Not given

4. Journalists frequently use cyber cafés.

- ☐ True
- ☐ False
- ☑ Not given

Prime Time 5. Testen und Fördern, Arbeitsheft (ISBN 978-3-209-08441-5)

Testen und Fördern

5. Yon says that the laptop is easier to use on a trip.

- ☐ True
- ☐ False
- ☑ **Not given**

6. She exclusively uses the computer to stay in contact with business partners.

- ☐ True
- ☑ **False**
- ☐ Not given

7. None of her children use the computer for school.

- ☐ True
- ☑ **False**
- ☐ Not given

8. 25% of all people in South Korea have high-speed Internet access.

- ☑ **True**
- ☐ False
- ☐ Not given

Prime Time 5. Testen und Fördern, Arbeitsheft (ISBN 978-3-209-08441-5)

1. Listening: Catching up on the phone

You will hear a telephone conversation in which George talks to Emily. For questions 1–5, choose the answer that fits best according to what you hear.

1. Where did Emily do her internship?

- ☐ England
- ☑ **Scotland**
- ☐ Wales
- ☐ Ireland

2. What do you learn about Sarah's job situation?

- ☐ She wants to change jobs.
- ☐ She wants to work for another company.
- ☐ She is very unhappy with her old job.
- ☑ **She is about to get a promotion.**

Testen und Fördern

3. What does George think about his son's new hobby?

- ☐ He is impressed by his son's talent.
- ☐ He refuses to pay for his son's guitar lessons.
- ☑ **He thinks that his son needs to practise.**
- ☐ He is sure his son will be a rockstar soon.

4. What is Emily's opinion about Mary's relationship?

- ☑ **She thinks that there is no reason to worry.**
- ☐ She thinks that Mary should be more responsible.
- ☐ She thinks that George should not accept it.
- ☐ She thinks that Mary is still too young.

5. According to the conversation, who is Sarah?

- ☐ George's sister
- ☐ Emily's best friend
- ☐ Emily's sister
- ☑ **George's wife**

Prime Time 5. Testen und Fördern, Arbeitsheft (ISBN 978-3-209-08441-5)

Testen und Fördern

Tapescript: Catching up on the phone

George	Hello?
Emily	This is Emily speaking.
George	Emily? Emily who?
Emily	George, don't be stupid!
George	Just kidding!! Great to hear from you! How are you doing?
Emily	I am doing wonderful, thank you!
George	Wow, it's been a long time ....
Emily	True! It's great being back in Ireland.
George	How was Scotland?
Emily	Scotland was awesome. I really enjoyed the internship at Brooks and Brothers. I met very nice people who showed me around. We even made a few trips to various places, both in England and in Wales.
George	When did you come back?
Emily	I arrived here only two days ago, and I have had so much to do since then.
George	I can imagine. You have been gone for 2 months, right?
Emily	Yes, and it's been a fantastic experience. More about that some other time, though … . What's more important … I'm calling because I'd like to catch up and see what's new!
George	Nothing much.
Emily	How's Sarah?
George	She's doing great. She is going to be promoted.
Emily	Wow, that's cool.
George	Yup, her boss came to her office the other day and told her about a higher position that needs to be filled. She couldn't believe it at first but now she already loves the idea of having more responsibility.
Emily	And what about the kids?
George	Well, Jeremy … he is doing well at school and pretty busy with his extracurricular activities.
Emily	What is he into at the moment? I just know that about 6 months ago he liked track and field. And he was rather good at it too, right?
George	Actually, yes, he was even part of the school's track and field team. But you know how kids are. Their interests change from one day to the next. Now he has taken up playing the guitar and has joined the school band. I even had to arrange for a private teacher. So far he mainly produces noise if you ask me.
Emily	(Hahahaha) You are the worst father ever. ☺
George	No, seriously, he is a great kid. And Mary … she has got a boyfriend now.
Emily	Hey, that's exciting.

Testen und Fördern

George	But she is only 15 … .
Emily	Which is old enough!
George	I don't think so.
Emily	I am sure he is a nice guy.
George	Maybe, but she is still too young to have a boyfriend!!
Emily	I wouldn't say so, I am sure she is a responsible girl.
George	I hope so …. Oh, by the way, have you heard about Lucy?
Emily	No, what's new with her?
George	She and Greg are going to have a baby.
Emily	Really?? I have to call her right away!
George	Yeah, you should. So when are the two of us going to get together?
Emily	On the weekend would be good for me.
George	Okay, I will talk to Sarah about it. Maybe we can have a barbecue at our place.
Emily	That sounds good. Looking forward to that. Bye!
George	Talk to you later. Bye!

Prime Time 5. Testen und Fördern, Arbeitsheft (ISBN 978-3-209-08441-5)

2. Listening: Today's fashion designers

You will hear part of a podcast in which Alyssa talks about today's fashion designers. For statements 1–6, choose the answer (True or False) that fits best according to what you hear.

1. The programme is called UCF podcasts.

- ☐ True
- ☑ **False**

2. Pop stars have not always decided what is fashionable.

- ☑ **True**
- ☐ False

3. Sheryl can afford designer clothes.

- ☐ True
- ☑ **False**

Testen und Fördern

4. Celebrities design their own clothes because they want their fans to feel more like them.

- ☐ True
- ☑ **False**

5. More and more pop stars worry that they will not stay popular for a long time.

- ☑ **True**
- ☐ False

6. The report explains the importance of stars in fashion.

- ☑ **True**
- ☐ False

Prime Time 5. Testen und Fördern, Arbeitsheft (ISBN 978-3-209-08441-5)

Testen und Fördern

Tapescript: Today's fashion designers

Hello, I'm Alyssa and you're listening to USF podcasts. Today's programme is on one of the most important aspects of life … at least for women (*chuckle*).

Lagerfeld, Calvin Klein, Versace … who's that? ☺ It often seems like these names were yesterday. Today it's stars like Paris Hilton, Miley Cyrus and David Beckham who make fashion and set trends.

The question is why pop stars and celebrities are now determining what's in and what's out. With their own clothing labels they set the tone for what people wear. For several generations, Madonna, for example, has been among the most popular and influential stars lots of normal people want to be like. Let's hear from Sheryl, a university student, what she thinks about pop stars going fashion.

(Sheryl) "*Well, I don't have a lot of money to spend on clothes but I sure like shopping. Of course I also wanna follow trends and keep my closet up to date. I think it's great that stars start their own labels because their clothes are usually affordable. If you think of the traditional designers … what they come up with is generally more expensive and most of the time not made for everyday clothing. When I buy clothes designed by celebrities … I have to say that I sometimes feel at least a bit like them. And that's a cool feeling.*"

While many consumers consider it a cool move, the stars may have various, sometimes even selfish, reasons for getting into the fashion business. First of all, there's a lot of money in that. Working with stores like H&M you reach millions of people, all wanting to wear what you supposedly wear. Another reason may be their wish to be even more famous than they already are. A pop star's career can be over within months, especially with all those casting shows going on nowadays. To keep their faces in the media and stay famous, stars often explore other areas. Fashion editor Linda Midway explains celebrities' marketing strategies:

(Linda) "*Famous people like Christina Aguilera and Beyoncé as well as the Becks can be considered marketing geniuses. They do not only sell their talent but their entire persona. Fans check out their hairstyle, their jewellery, their accessories and, of course, their clothes. People like Paris Hilton know how to build a business empire based on them advertising themselves.*"

The most likely explanation for stars being really successful as designers is that they produce clothes for the masses, for the boys and girls next door.

This is Alyssa and I'll be back with more entertainment news next week.

◄ ↔┘

Testen und Fördern

3. Reading: Less sugar in Kellogg's cereals

You are going to read a text about a change in Kellogg's cereals. For statements 1–7, choose the answer (True, False or Not given) which fits best according to what you read.

Kellogg's is reacting to several claims that cereals, which show high levels of sugar, salt and fat, can contribute to childhood obesity. Kellogg's UK managing director Greg Peterson says that they are more than willing to act upon lots of mothers' wishes for tasty cereals with low sugar content. Changing four of Kellogg's Coco Pops products in the next year will be the first step towards a future of healthier cereals.

At the moment Coco Pops contain about 35% sugar. Having invested a lot of money and staff hours in the course of the past two years, Kellogg's will soon manage to reduce the sugar content to approximately 29%, which will, however, still be almost twice the amount recommended by the Food Standards Agency.

Lucy Jones, a member of the British Dietetic Association, confirms that Kellogg's has at least made a small move in the right direction and by doing so is clearly following a trend of sugar, salt and fat reductions in food. Salt levels in particular have fallen a great deal in various products in the past few years. However, Jones also points out that further reductions in sugar will be necessary in the future since sugar does not only affect the people's weight management but also their teeth and blood glucose levels.

With Kellogg's being among the most popular cereal producers, many parents appreciate this change in the quality of Kellogg's products. In the UK, for example, four out of ten people have at least one box of Coco Pops at home. Considering nutritionists' claim that breakfast is the most important meal of the day, health-conscious parents who want their children to have breakfast are, naturally, eager to put something healthy and at the same time tasty on the table.

Several studies have proven the importance of having breakfast. Starting the day without it can have a negative influence on people's concentration and energy levels and, in the long run, also lead to weight problems.

Greg Peterson has confirmed Kellogg's' intention to keep reducing sugar levels in the future if they can maintain the quality of the product taste.

◄ ↕‡

Prime Time 5. Testen und Fördern, Arbeitsheft (ISBN 978-3-209-08441-5)

Testen und Fördern

1. Kellogg's will reduce the sugar content of all Kellogg's Coco Pops products in the next year.

- ☐ True
- ☑ **False**
- ☐ Not given

2. Kellogg's spent a small amount of money on the product's quality.

- ☐ True
- ☑ **False**
- ☐ Not given

3. The Food Standards Agency does not recommend Kellogg's products.

- ☐ True
- ☐ False
- ☑ **Not given**

4. Lucy Jones welcomes the changes Kellogg's has made.

- ☑ **True**
- ☐ False
- ☐ Not given

Testen und Fördern

5. According to the text, high sugar levels only cause weight problems.

- ☐ True
- ☑ **False**
- ☐ Not given

6. 40% of all consumers in the UK buy Kellogg's products.

- ☑ **True**
- ☐ False
- ☐ Not given

7. People usually are in a better mood after having breakfast.

- ☐ True
- ☐ False
- ☑ **Not given**

Prime Time 5. Testen und Fördern, Arbeitsheft (ISBN 978-3-209-08441-5)

4. Reading: Summer Jobs

You are going to read a text on summer jobs. For questions 1–5, choose the answer which fits best according to what you read.

During the summer holidays a lot of teenagers decide to take on a job. As soon as you reach the age of 15, you have the permission to work in your holidays. Going to work means taking over new responsibilities, following orders and also getting up early, which does not always appeal to young people. However, summer jobs have attractive benefits. After learning about the following three reasons for getting yourself a job we are sure you will want to go out and find one.

Work experience

Summer jobs are a great opportunity to get to know various work fields. Acquiring useful skills and gaining knowledge about all sorts of working processes is only one of many advantages. If you realize that the line of work you have chosen is not the right one for you, just remember that the time you spend at a summer job is limited. Finding out about your likes and dislikes will help you plan your future. In addition to the work experience, you also get the chance to work on your self-confidence and feel good about yourself.

Teamwork

No matter whether you work at a gas station, in an office or a supermarket, you always work together with other people. Working in a team can be a challenge because you cannot only think about your own needs, you also have to accept the opinions of others. You must be ready to share your ideas, help others out and show understanding for your fellow colleagues. Today being able to work in a team often decides whether you get a job or not.

Money

Another very attractive advantage of spending your summer holidays working is the money you earn. In Austria teenagers usually make between 600 and 1,000 Euros per month. Making your own money gives you a feeling of independence from your parents. In addition, you can afford bigger expenses like paying for your driver's license or a new computer.

Of course, you could spend your holidays sitting on the couch at home, playing computer games or watching TV all day long but this will not get you anywhere. So write your application, go to the interview, get the job and set your alarm: It's time to leave for work and conquer the world.

1. Why do teenagers only start doing summer jobs at the age of 15?

☐ Younger teenagers are not responsible enough before that.
☐ Younger teenagers do not want to get up that early.
☑ **Younger teenagers are not allowed to take a job.**

2. Why is it sometimes good that summer jobs only last for a few weeks?

☐ Because you learn new things very quickly.
☑ **Because you might have to do something you don't like.**
☐ Because you can still enjoy part of your holiday.

3. What makes working in a team a challenge?

☐ Your needs are less important than your colleagues' needs.
☑ **You should be willing to deal with other people's views.**
☐ You always have to come up with new ideas.

Prime Time 5. Testen und Fördern, Arbeitsheft (ISBN 978-3-209-08441-5)

Testen und Fördern

4. According to the text, what is meant by the word "expenses"?

- ☐ the money you save
- ☐ the money you earn
- ☒ **the money you spend**

5. What do the authors of this text want you to do?

- ☒ **get work experience**
- ☐ earn a lot of money
- ☐ plan your future

1. Listening: Boys at school

You will hear part of a radio interview with 15-year-old Bill about school. For questions 1–5, choose the answer which fits best according to what you hear.

1. What have recent studies shown?

- ☐ Girls are as good as boys at school.
- ☐ Boys do better at school than girls.
- ☑ **Girls produce better results than boys.**

2. When will the School Improvement Officer be on air?

- ☑ **the next day**
- ☐ later that day
- ☐ some time next week

Testen und Fördern

3. In secondary school, how did Bill deal with his workload?

- ☐ He did not work hard enough.
- ☐ He gave up quickly.
- ☑ **He tried to manage the pressure.**

4. How did his bad marks affect his opinion about school?

- ☐ They did not affect his opinion at all.
- ☑ **He started to dislike school.**
- ☐ He was annoyed by his teachers' reaction.

5. Was Bill the only boy in his class with problems?

- ☐ There were a few boys facing the same problems.
- ☐ Bill was the one having the biggest problems.
- ☑ **Most of the boys in his class had the same problems.**

Prime Time 5. Testen und Fördern, Arbeitsheft (ISBN 978-3-209-08441-5)

Tapescript: Boys at school

Radio	With education becoming more and more important in today's world, educators, test developers and politicians take a very close look at the students' performance at any stage of a student's educational career. Recent research has once again shown that, looking at the gender gap, girls clearly outperform boys at school. Boys have got considerable learning difficulties and struggle to succeed in reading and writing. The situation is actually alarming and asks for more attention. Before we will have the chance to talk to a UK school improvement officer in tomorrow's show, we have been able to invite Bill, a 15-year-old boy from Kent, who will share his story with us today. Welcome, Bill!
Bill	Thank you, John. I am happy to be here today.
Radio	Tell us a little bit about your school career.
Bill	Well, I didn't start out too great actually. In primary school, things seemed to be fine and I was doing okay. But as soon as I attended secondary school, problems began to arise.
Radio	What kind of problems?
Bill	I quickly ran into problems in all the language subjects and also in some of the natural science subjects. Although I tried to stay on top of my workload, it seemed impossible to keep up after a short while and I soon got very bad marks on tests as well as exams.
Radio	How did you feel about this?
Bill	I felt helpless. My parents didn't know what to do either. Private tutoring also didn't work and all this frustration finally led to a very negative attitude towards school.
Radio	Did your teachers talk to you or give you any advice?
Bill	Some tried to, but when they eventually realized what was going on, it was almost too late, to be honest.
Radio	Were you the only one in your class experiencing such difficulties?
Bill	In fact, there were only a few exceptions who didn't have any problems. This was the reason why our teachers started to ask questions.
Radio	Did they only ask questions or was anything changed after you had shared your problems and worries with them?
Bill	Well, I have to say that our teachers took our problems really seriously. After a few weeks of discussion and project work we all came up with new methods that helped us to overcome our frustrations.
Radio	What did your teachers change, for example?
Bill	First of all, they paid close attention to our seating arrangements. You could finally see boys sitting everywhere in the classroom, not only in the back row. They also tried to find topics that were interesting to all the students in the class.
Radio	Bill, thank you very much for now. Stay tuned for more information after the break … (fade out)

E8 Listening Strategies

(http://www.uni-klu.ac.at/ltc/downloads/LTC_Technical_Report_3.pdf)

1. **1.2.** Listening for main idea(s) or important information and distinguishing that from supporting detail or examples. This includes distinguishing fact from opinion when clearly marked.
2. **1.3.** Listening for specific information, including recall of important details. Understanding directions and instructions.
3. **1.2.** Listening for main idea(s) or important information and distinguishing that from supporting detail or examples. This includes distinguishing fact from opinion when clearly marked.
4. **2.1.** Making inferences and deductions based on information in the text. This can include deducing meaning of unfamiliar lexical items from context.
5. **1.2.** Listening for main idea(s) or important information and distinguishing that from supporting detail or examples. This includes distinguishing fact from opinion when clearly marked.

BIST Deskriptoren – HÖREN

Die Schülerinnen und Schüler können
einfachen Interviews, Berichten, Hörspielen und Sketches zu vertrauten Themen folgen (B1).

GERS Beschreibung – Hörverstehen allgemein

B1 Kann unkomplizierte Sachinformationen über gewöhnliche alltags- oder berufsbezogene Themen verstehen und dabei die Hauptaussagen und Einzelinformationen erkennen, sofern klar artikuliert und mit vertrautem Akzent gesprochen wird.

Themenbereich(e):

Schule und Arbeitswelt

Prime Time 5. Testen und Fördern, Arbeitsheft (ISBN 978-3-209-08441-5)

2. Listening: Hip hop

You will hear part of a radio interview about hip hop. For statements 1–7, choose the answer (True or False) which fits best according to what you hear.

1. The radio guest's name is Karen Easton.

- ☐ True
- ☑ **False**

2. Hip hop started in one particular area of New York City.

- ☑ **True**
- ☐ False

3. In hip hop five stylistic elements are mixed together.

- ☐ True
- ☑ **False**

Testen und Fördern

4. Hip hop is not the same as rap.

- ☐ True
- ☑ **False**

5. A lot of music genres come from African music.

- ☑ **True**
- ☐ False

6. The radio guest Karen is not coming back after the break.

- ☐ True
- ☑ **False**

7. The people at block parties liked funk and soul music.

- ☑ **True**
- ☐ False

Prime Time 5. Testen und Fördern, Arbeitsheft (ISBN 978-3-209-08441-5)

Testen und Fördern

Tapescript: Hip hop

George	Welcome to our weekly "Music rocks" show. This is George Mally on FM 5. It's time to learn about another style of music. Jazz was what we talked about last week. This week we would like to dedicate to hip hop. Hip hop! What is it? … Where does it come from? … Why do people like it? (*pause*) With me today is Karen East, an expert on the origins of hip hop and its importance in today's music business. Welcome, Karen!
Karen	Thank you, George. It's a pleasure to be here.
George	So, tell me Karen, what is hip hop, and more importantly, where does it come from?
Karen	Well, hip hop music is a musical genre that is actually part of the hip hop culture. It began in New York City, more specifically in the South Bronx of New York City.
George	When was that?
Karen	In the 1970s.
George	So hip hop has been around for a while.
Karen	Quite a while, yes …
George	If you had to describe hip hop as a musical genre, what would you say?
Karen	Well … In hip hop several stylistic elements are mixed together. One of them is rapping, of course. Then there is DJing, which is also referred to as scratching, sampling and, finally, beatboxing.
George	I always thought hip hop and rap were two different things.
Karen	Well, you can actually use the term "rap" as a synonym for hip hop. I have to add, however, that hip hop does not only stand for a certain type of music but for a whole subculture and its way of thinking and living.
George	OK … then what can you tell us about rapping?
Karen	Rapping is speaking lyrically, in rhyme and verse. Usually there's some sort of beat supporting or accompanying the rap.
George	And what about the origins of hip hop?
Karen	Its roots can be found in African-American music and African music, which is the case with quite a number of music genres actually.
George	Now, … in the beginning you said that hip hop has been around since the 1970s. Could you give us a little bit of insight into the early days of hip hop before we say goodbye to our listeners for a quick commercial break.
Karen	Of course … It all started when block parties became more and more popular in New York. At these parties, DJs usually played funk and soul music, which was received very well by the audience. As a consequence of the positive reaction, DJs started experimenting a little. Isolating the percussion breaks of well-known songs was actually the first step.
George	Hip hop – a music genre widely spread today! We've only just started talking about its development. After the break we'll go on a quick but informative trip through time, starting in the 1970s up until the 21st century and hear a lot about its importance in the business today. If you have any particular questions, feel free to call or email us. You can also visit us on Facebook and post a question or comment.

◄↕↵

Testen und Fördern

E8 Listening Strategies

(http://www.uni-klu.ac.at/ltc/downloads/LTC_Technical_Report_3.pdf)

1. **1.3.** Listening for specific information, including recall of important details. Understanding directions and instructions.
2. **1.3.** Listening for specific information, including recall of important details. Understanding directions and instructions
3. **1.3.** Listening for specific information, including recall of important details. Understanding directions and instructions
4. **1.2.** Listening for main idea(s) or important information and distinguishing that from supporting detail or examples. This includes distinguishing fact from opinion when clearly marked.
5. **1.3.** Listening for specific information, including recall of important details. Understanding directions and instructions.
6. **2.1.** Making inferences and deductions based on information in the text. This can include deducing meaning of unfamiliar lexical items from context.
7. **1.2.** Listening for main idea(s) or important information and distinguishing that from supporting detail or examples. This includes distinguishing fact from opinion when clearly marked.

BIST Deskriptoren – HÖREN

Die Schülerinnen und Schüler können

einfachen Interviews, Berichten, Hörspielen und Sketches zu vertrauten Themen folgen (B1).

GERS Beschreibung – Hörverstehen allgemein

B1 Kann unkomplizierte Sachinformationen über gewöhnliche alltags- oder berufsbezogene Themen verstehen und dabei die Hauptaussagen und Einzelinformationen erkennen, sofern klar artikuliert und mit vertrautem Akzent gesprochen wird.

Themenbereich(e):

Kultur, Medien und Literatur

◄↕↵

Prime Time 5. Testen und Fördern, Arbeitsheft (ISBN 978-3-209-08441-5)

3. Reading: Package holidays

You are going to read a text on package holidays. For questions 1–5, choose the answer which fits best according to what you read.

Package holidays

Package holidays, also known as package tours, are a holiday combination of transport and accommodation generally geared toward travelers favoring mass tourism. These package holidays usually include services like a rental car or different sorts of activities or trips during the holidays. They are generally organized by tour operators, and marketed and sold to consumers by travel agents. While some travel agents work for tour operators, others are independent.

In the majority of cases, tourists make use of charter airlines to travel to foreign countries. Flights provided on a charter basis are generally more expensive but at the same time more convenient for travelers because they operate outside normal schedules.

Thomas Cook was the first person to offer a package tour of Europe in 1855 after organizing what could be considered an early form of package holiday in 1841, namely a return trip between Leicester and Loughborough. By the beginning of the 1870s, Cook was in the position to offer tours all over the world, but only for small groups of tourists.

Vladimir Raitz, co-founder of the Horizon Holiday Group and father of the modern British package holiday, pioneered mass package holidays abroad via charter airlines. In 1950, he offered an all-inclusive holiday in Corsica, departing from Gatwick airport. Eleven paying customers took part in his inaugural flight and enjoyed a holiday consisting of a return ticket, tented accommodation on the beach and tasty food.

At the time, a return flight to Nice, for instance, was £70, the equivalent of approximately £1.700 these days. In the 1960s, only ten years after the first mass package holiday had been offered, more and more people in the UK could afford to travel abroad, always enjoying a well-prepared combination of flight, transfers and accommodation.

At the beginning of the twenty-first century, travelers started avoiding package holidays and concentrating on traveling with budget airlines and taking care of their accommodation themselves. In the UK, the decline in package holidays resulted in the consolidation of the tour operator market, which is now ruled by a few big tour operators, including Thomson Holidays, Thomas Cook AG and First Choice.

As a considerable number of flight and holiday companies filed for bankruptcy and the hidden costs of no-frills flights – such as extra charge for heavy baggage or check-in at the airport instead of online check-in – kept increasing, travelers wanted financial security, which helped package holidays see a new boost in 2009. An increase in last-minute bookings has also made package holidays more popular again.

1. What role do travel agents play with regard to package holidays?

- ☐ They exclusively work for tour operators.
- ☐ They organize package holidays.
- ☑ **They offer package holidays.**

2. What is the main benefit of charter flights?

- ☑ **They are more flexible.**
- ☐ They follow normal schedules.
- ☐ They are cheaper.

3. "Vladimir Raitz […] pioneered mass package holidays abroad via charter airlines." What does "*pioneer*" mean in this context?

- ☐ He was the first to transport package holiday travelers.
- ☐ He was the first to offer all-inclusive holidays.
- ☑ **He was the first to organize package holidays for large groups.**

4. What led to a decrease in package holidays at the beginning of the new millennium?

- ☐ The market was controlled by a small number of big tour operators.
- ☑ **Tourists took more action in organizing their own holidays.**
- ☐ The number of budget airlines offering cheap flights increased.

Prime Time 5. Testen und Fördern, Arbeitsheft (ISBN 978-3-209-08441-5)

5. Why did travelers return to booking package holidays a few years later?

☐ Because many holiday companies and airlines closed down.

☐ Because package holidays had become cheaper.

☑ **Because package holidays did not produce additional costs.**

Testen und Fördern

E8 Reading Strategies
(http://www.uni-klu.ac.at/ltc/downloads/LTC_Technical_Report_2.pdf)

1. **3.2.** Locating, identifying, understanding and comparing facts, opinions, definitions (search reading included).
2. **3.1.** Understanding explicitly stated main idea(s) and/or distinguishing that from supporting details.
3. **3.2.** Locating, identifying, understanding and comparing facts, opinions, definitions (search reading included).
4. **3.5.** Making propositional inferences (deducing information that is not explicitly stated from information that is explicitly stated).
5. **3.1.** Understanding explicitly stated main idea(s) and/or distinguishing that from supporting details.

BIST Deskriptoren – LESEN
Die Schülerinnen und Schüler können
unkomplizierte Sachtexte über Themen, die mit den eigenen Interessen und Fachgebieten aus den Themenbereichen des Lehrplans in Zusammenhang stehen, mit befriedigendem Verständnis lesen (B1).

GERS Beschreibung – Leseverstehen allgemein
B1 Kann unkomplizierte Sachtexte über Themen, die mit den eigenen Interessen und Fachgebieten in Zusammenhang stehen, mit befriedigendem Verständnis lesen.

Themenbereich(e):
Umwelt und Gesellschaft

Prime Time 5. Testen und Fördern, Arbeitsheft (ISBN 978-3-209-08441-5)

4. Reading: Eating disorders in teenagers

You are going to read a text on eating disorders in teenagers. For statements 1–6, choose the answer (True or False) which fits best according to what you read.

Eating disorders in teenagers

With the onset of puberty, children turn into teenagers and a period called adolescence begins. Adolescence is the time between puberty and young adulthood, in which the young human body undergoes important physical and mental changes.

To form the basis for normal development and growth, teenagers do not only need constant support, understanding and time to reflect on themselves and their actions, but also a lot of healthy high-quality food. Their bones grow quickly and, depending on the teenagers' growing needs, they should consume high calorie foods.

In Western society in particular, more and more teenagers harm their bodies instead of taking good care of them. One problem a great number of teenagers but also young adults are facing today are eating disorders, which affect the human body negatively. Eating disorders are now considered the third most common chronic disease, especially in young women. The number of people affected has been rising dramatically in the past three decades. If not treated as early as possible, complex illnesses may be a consequence.

An eating disorder, in general, is a condition characterised by abnormal eating behaviour that may involve either too little or too much food intake. While there are quite a number of different eating disorders, anorexia nervosa and bulimia nervosa are the most common ones in young people.

People who starve themselves suffer from anorexia nervosa. The weight loss such people experience is extreme and normally 15% below their normal body weight. The main problem with anorexic people is that, regardless of how thin they are, they always believe that they are too fat. Their fear of gaining weight makes them do excessive exercise, take in laxatives or refuse to eat at all.

Bulimia nervosa is an eating disorder characterised by a combination of refusing to eat and taking in loads of food in a very short period of time. Feelings of guilt, weakness and low self-esteem are often the result of excessive food intake. In order to compensate for these bad feelings, bulimic people try to get rid of the food they have eaten, either by throwing up or by using laxatives.

Teenagers suffering from eating disorders frequently have to deal with serious medical consequences, such as growth retardation, abnormal weight and pubertal delay. Girls in particular have to face irregular or even absent menstruation. Eating disorders can also lead to a loss of body fat, muscle mass as well as bone mineral when the human body is growing. Moreover, there might be abnormalities with regard to one's levels of vitamins, minerals and other trace elements. These problems do not go away when entering adulthood. In fact, they get worse.

Apart from the medical consequences, eating disorders go hand in hand with psychological and emotional problems. People, especially teenagers, suffering from eating disorders often isolate themselves. They also fall easy victim to feelings of anxiety, low self-worth and depression. Regardless of whether one addresses the physical or the psychological consequences of eating disorders, both of them are destructive and affect people's quality of life extremely negatively.

Testen und Fördern

1. Teenagers should avoid meals with a high calorie count.

☐ True
☑ **False**

2. The amount of people suffering from eating disorders is slowly increasing.

☐ True
☑ **False**

3. An eating disorder is connected to an excessive intake of food.

☐ True
☑ **False**

4. Anorexic people have a wrong image of their own body.

☑ **True**
☐ False

5. People suffering from eating disorders have more problems the older they get.

☑ **True**
☐ False

6. Bulimic and anorexic people often turn away from social contacts.

☑ **True**
☐ False

Prime Time 5. Testen und Fördern, Arbeitsheft (ISBN 978-3-209-08441-5)

5. Language in use: Job interviews

Read the text on job interviews. Some words are missing. Use the words in brackets to form words that fit in the gaps. Write your answers in the gaps.

When ***preparing*** (**prepare**) for a job interview, you need to know what the company is looking for. Interviewers want to employ people who are intelligent, flexible and able to work in a team. It is also important to be good at ***communicating*** (**communicate**) with others and expressing yourself clearly (**clear**).

Applicants (**Apply**) for a job are usually asked about their work experience and their education. Take every chance to gain ***knowledge*** (**know**) about the field you plan on working in. Summer jobs and unpaid internships often pay off later on.

Before going to the ***actual*** (**actual**) interview, make sure to do your research. You should know what the company does and who the most important people like managers and supervisors are. Moreover, think about what to wear. It is always good to be ***dressed*** (**dress**) smartly.

6. Language in use: Dear diary

Read the diary entry and choose the correct preposition for each gap. Write it in the gap.

Dear diary,

today has been the worst day ...*of*... (**from / of / in**) my life. You know Mary, my best friend. We have known each other ...*for*... (**over / since / for**) ages and we have never really had a fight before. Up to now! She did the most horrible thing ...*to*... (**to / for / at**) me that you can imagine. She really had the nerve to flirt ...*with*... (**about / with / at**) Tony, even though she knows that I am secretly in love ...*with*... (**toward / with / for**) him.

I had just entered the cafeteria when I saw them standing close ...*to*... (**next / around / to**) each other. I left without asking them what they were talking ...*about*... (**over / about / through**). I don't want to see her tomorrow! What if …

Testen und Fördern

E8 Reading Strategies

(http://www.uni-klu.ac.at/ltc/downloads/LTC_Technical_Report_2.pdf)

1. **3.1.** Understanding explicitly stated main idea(s) and/or distinguishing that from supporting details.
2. **3.2.** Locating, identifying, understanding and comparing facts, opinions, definitions (search reading included).
3. **3.1.** Understanding explicitly stated main idea(s) and/or distinguishing that from supporting details.
4. **3.5.** Making propositional inferences (deducing information that is not explicitly stated from information that is explicitly stated).
5. **3.2.** Locating, identifying, understanding and comparing facts, opinions, definitions (search reading included).
6. **3.1.** Understanding explicitly stated main idea(s) and/or distinguishing that from supporting details.

BIST Deskriptoren – LESEN

Die Schülerinnen und Schüler können

unkomplizierte Sachtexte über Themen, die mit den eigenen Interessen und Fachgebieten aus den Themenbereichen des Lehrplans in Zusammenhang stehen, mit befriedigendem Verständnis lesen (B1).

GERS Beschreibung – Leseverstehen allgemein

B1 Kann unkomplizierte Sachtexte über Themen, die mit den eigenen Interessen und Fachgebieten in Zusammenhang stehen, mit befriedigendem Verständnis lesen.

Themenbereich(e):

Koerper und Gesundheit

Prime Time 5. Testen und Fördern, Arbeitsheft (ISBN 978-3-209-08441-5)

Testen und Fördern

1. Listening: The Maitreya Project in India

You will hear part of a radio interview between Eric Clark and Bita Rina on the Maitreya Education Project in India. For questions 1-5, choose the answer which fits best according to what you hear.

1. What is Bita Rina's role in the Maitreya Project?

- ☐ She is a sponsor.
- ☐ She is the founder.
- ☑ **She is a representative.**

2. What does the project NOT focus on?

- ☐ healthcare
- ☑ **social welfare**
- ☐ infrastructure

3. Why is the project of great importance for that region?

- ☐ Because most people are unemployed.
- ☐ Because most people are badly educated.
- ☑ **Because most people need better medical treatment.**

Testen und Fördern

4. Under what condition will new schools be built?

- ☑ **Sponsors provide both money and locations.**
- ☐ There is a higher interest of children and adults in education.
- ☐ The curriculum covers a greater variety of subjects.

5. What is the "good heart"?

- ☐ a subject
- ☐ a project
- ☑ **a concept**

Prime Time 5. Testen und Fördern, Arbeitsheft (ISBN 978-3-209-08441-5)

Tapescript: The Maitreya Project in India

Radio	It's two o'clock in the afternoon and this is Eric Clark with 'Education worldwide'. It is a great pleasure to welcome Bita Rina today, a representative of the Maitreya Project in northern India which is sponsored by our radio station. …. Welcome Ms Rina!
Rina	Thank you very much for inviting me. It's great to be here.
Radio	Please tell us something about the Maitreya Project.
Rina	The Maitreya Project is a multi-faceted project including all sorts of programs with regard to infrastructure, employment, healthcare and, of course, education. Especially by introducing extensive education and healthcare programs of high quality and, what's even more significant, of international standards, we hope to contribute to the people's well-being in the region.
Radio	I suppose there is an urgent need for such a program particularly in this region?
Rina	Millions of people living in the rural areas of northern India have to cope with extremely difficult circumstances. Most of the people living there do not receive adequate healthcare. There are also people who receive no healthcare whatsoever because they cannot afford it. Malnourishment, a high rate of infant mortality and poor health are part of everyday life.
Radio	Could you give us a bit more insight into your mission?
Rina	We have defined various missions for the project. Offering medical services, both to cure as well as to prevent diseases, and health education for children and grown-ups is just one aspect of the program. In terms of education, a curriculum has been developed which aims at academic achievement and moral development. Depending on funding and the availability of land sites, new schools will be built, which will then provide primary, secondary and even vocational education.
Radio	As far as I am informed, you are also planning to have an impact on the employment and infrastructural development in the area.
Rina	Yes, that's true.
Radio	I have to say I am very impressed by what I've heard so far. If you don't mind I would like to learn more about the Maitreya **Education** Project, its curriculum, subjects and social implications.
Rina	I'd love to say more about our education project. I am really grateful we are in the position to provide free education from kindergarten to secondary school to all village children, no matter what their religion, caste, gender or social status. Our curriculum is based on "the good heart".
Radio	What do you mean by "the good heart"?
Rina	The idea of "the good heart" is about the qualities of kindness and compassion. We help our children develop a sense of respect and ethical responsibility towards other beings.
Radio	Interesting. (*pause*) Thank you so much for the insight you have already provided. After the break we will be back with more information on the Maitreya Education Project. You are also welcome to call and ask questions concerning Bita Rina's work in India. (*fade out*)

E8 Listening Strategies

(http://www.uni-klu.ac.at/ltc/downloads/LTC_Technical_Report_3.pdf)

1. **1.3.** Listening for specific information, including recall of important details. Understanding directions and instructions.
2. **1.3.** Listening for specific information, including recall of important details. Understanding directions and instructions.
3. **1.2.** Listening for main idea(s) or important information and distinguishing that from supporting detail or examples. This includes distinguishing fact from opinion when clearly marked.
4. **1.2.** Listening for main idea(s) or important information and distinguishing that from supporting detail or examples. This includes distinguishing fact from opinion when clearly marked.
5. **2.1.** Making inferences and deductions based on information in the text. This can include deducing meaning of unfamiliar lexical items from context.

BIST Deskriptoren – HÖREN

Die Schülerinnen und Schüler können

einfachen Interviews, Berichten, Hörspielen und Sketches zu vertrauten Themen folgen (B1).

GERS Beschreibung – Hörverstehen allgemein

B1 Kann unkomplizierte Sachinformationen über gewöhnliche alltags- oder berufsbezogene Themen verstehen und dabei die Hauptaussagen und Einzelinformationen erkennen, sofern klar artikuliert und mit vertrautem Akzent gesprochen wird.

Themenbereich(e):

Interkulturelle und landeskundliche Aspekte

Prime Time 5. Testen und Fördern, Arbeitsheft (ISBN 978-3-209-08441-5)

2. Listening: Mice

You will hear a radio report about mice. For statements 1-7, choose the answer (True or False) which fits best according to what you hear.

1. The field mouse is the best-known mouse species.

- ☐ True
- ☑ **False**

2. Despite their many natural enemies, mice can live in nearly all areas.

- ☑ **True**
- ☐ False

3. Mice are carriers of illnesses.

- ☑ **True**
- ☐ False

Testen und Fördern

4. Mice are most active during the day.

- ☐ True
- ☑ **False**

5. Mice can see as well as they can hear.

- ☐ True
- ☑ **False**

6. Mice are often used in labs although they are expensive.

- ☐ True
- ☑ **False**

7. Mice easily adapt around humans.

- ☑ **True**
- ☐ False

Prime Time 5. Testen und Fördern, Arbeitsheft (ISBN 978-3-209-08441-5)

Tapescript: Mice

Mice are small mammals that belong to the order of rodents. The best-known mouse species is the house mouse, which is often kept as a pet. In some places, people are also familiar with different sorts of field mice.

Cats, wild dogs, foxes, birds of prey and snakes are known to feed on mice. Even though it has its enemies, which prey heavily upon it, the mouse is among the most successful mammals in the world today. Its most remarkable feature is its ability to adapt to all kinds of environments.

Mice can be extremely harmful and annoying rodents. They may damage and eat crops or spread diseases through their feces and parasites.

Mice are nocturnal animals. While they have a well-developed sense of hearing, their eyesight is very poor. Their sense of smell helps them find food and spot predators.

Mice are often used for experiments in the fields of biology and psychology, on the one hand because they are mammals and on the other hand because their gene material is similar to humans. Compared to rats, mice are used more frequently in scientific experiments. Other reasons for making use of mice in labs are that they are tiny, inexpensive and that they reproduce quickly.

Pet mice are popular with both children and teenagers. They can be good companions because they like to play and because it does not take them long to get used to humans. Owners of pet mice should not leave their mice unattended outside. Natural predators such as birds, lizards, dogs and cats are just waiting for some nice and tasty snack.

In case you are thinking about getting a pet mouse, make sure that you have a big enough cage. It should be about the size of a hamster cage. Mice normally eat any kind of fruit or grain from plants. When you keep a mouse, you can also buy food for it in a pet store.

E8 Listening Strategies

(http://www.uni-klu.ac.at/ltc/downloads/LTC_Technical_Report_3.pdf)

1. **1.2.** Listening for main idea(s) or important information and distinguishing that from supporting detail or examples. This includes distinguishing fact from opinion when clearly marked
2. **1.3.** Listening for specific information, including recall of important details. Understanding directions and instructions.
3. **1.2.** Listening for main idea(s) or important information and distinguishing that from supporting detail or examples. This includes distinguishing fact from opinion when clearly marked.
4. **1.3.** Listening for specific information, including recall of important details. Understanding directions and instructions.
5. **1.2.** Listening for main idea(s) or important information and distinguishing that from supporting detail or examples. This includes distinguishing fact from opinion when clearly marked.
6. **1.2.** Listening for main idea(s) or important information and distinguishing that from supporting detail or examples. This includes distinguishing fact from opinion when clearly marked
7. **1.2.** Listening for main idea(s) or important information and distinguishing that from supporting detail or examples. This includes distinguishing fact from opinion when clearly marked.

BIST Deskriptoren – HÖREN

Die Schülerinnen und Schüler können

einfachen Interviews, Berichten, Hörspielen und Sketches zu vertrauten Themen folgen (B1).

GERS Beschreibung – Hörverstehen allgemein

B1 Kann unkomplizierte Sachinformationen über gewöhnliche alltags- oder berufsbezogene Themen verstehen und dabei die Hauptaussagen und Einzelinformationen erkennen, sofern klar artikuliert und mit vertrautem Akzent gesprochen wird.

Themenbereich(e):

Umwelt und Gesellschaft

Prime Time 5. Testen und Fördern, Arbeitsheft (ISBN 978-3-209-08441-5)

3. Reading: The importance of reading

You are going to read a text on the importance of reading. For questions 1-5, choose the answer which fits best according to what you read.

The importance of reading

Being able to read is one of the most valuable skills to be acquired because it opens the doors to infinite knowledge and changes our view of the world and of the people who live in it. The skill of reading therefore plays an important role in an individual's personal and educational development.

Although used throughout in education, more and more people do not consider reading a pleasant free-time activity. For young people especially, reading often becomes an imposition, something that they would like to avoid if at all possible. One reason for people losing interest in reading is the availability of all sorts of media which seem to be far more attractive these days because they often do not ask for being active. A growing number of young people, children and teenagers alike, prefer spending their time playing computer games or watching television. Adults often busy themselves with work or seemingly more exciting leisure time activities too.

People who understand the importance of reading keep pointing out how crucial it is that we do not stop reading but that we learn to appreciate the benefit of it. Children in particular need to be made familiar with books and their advantages from an early age.

There are various reasons why reading is of high significance to us. Children who are read to – or read themselves as soon as they are able to – develop a greater ability of understanding different concepts without much effort. Their critical thinking benefits from the stories they are confronted with. Generally, it can be said that they learn how to think independently instead of being constantly spoon-fed.

The equation is an easy one: The more children read, the better they become at reading. The more interesting and enjoyable the texts they read are, the more they will want to read in general. Furthermore, by reading children automatically build their vocabulary and improve their command of language as well as of their communication skills. By reading children are exposed to a great variety of grammatical structures and phrases. In addition, being good at reading has an immediate effect on their spoken and written language skills.

What people have to begin to understand is that reading does not have to be considered annoying or tiresome. Pick the right book or text and you will experience quite the opposite! Reading enriches people's lives because it allows them to lose themselves in different worlds – their own worlds of imagination – and to gain knowledge of everything one can possibly think about.

It is the ability to evaluate, process and question the world we live in that makes us stand out from the rest. By giving up reading we give up an important part of our independence!

1. What is meant by "imposition" in the second paragraph?

- ☐ an activity
- ☐ a benefit
- ☑ **a hardship**

2. Who likes spending their time with things other than reading?

- ☐ children and teenagers
- ☐ children and adults
- ☑ **children, teenagers and adults**

3. "People who understand the importance of reading keep pointing out how crucial it is that we do not stop reading but that we learn to appreciate the benefit of it." What does "it" at the end of the sentence refer to?

- ☐ importance
- ☑ **reading**
- ☐ benefit

4. When should children be made familiar with books?

- ☑ **before they can read**
- ☐ as soon as they can read
- ☐ when they understand the books

5. What makes people like reading?

- ☐ They improve their grammatical knowledge.
- ☐ They develop their communication skills.
- ☑ **They are interested in the stories.**

Prime Time 5. Testen und Fördern, Arbeitsheft (ISBN 978-3-209-08441-5)

E8 Reading Strategies

(http://www.uni-klu.ac.at/ltc/downloads/LTC_Technical_Report_2.pdf)

1. **4.1.** Predicting the meaning of (unknown) words from the context.
2. **3.2.** Locating, identifying, understanding and comparing facts, opinions, definitions (search reading included).
3. **3.4.** Understanding cohesive relationships (reference, ellipsis, substitution, conjunction, lexical cohesion)
4. **3.1.** Understanding explicitly stated main idea(s) and/or distinguishing that from supporting details.
5. **3.1.** Understanding explicitly stated main idea(s) and/or distinguishing that from supporting details.

BIST Deskriptoren – LESEN

Die Schülerinnen und Schüler können

unkomplizierte Sachtexte über Themen, die mit den eigenen Interessen und Fachgebieten aus den Themenbereichen des Lehrplans in Zusammenhang stehen, mit befriedigendem Verständnis lesen (B1).

GERS Beschreibung – Leseverstehen allgemein

B1 Kann unkomplizierte Sachtexte über Themen, die mit den eigenen Interessen und Fachgebieten in Zusammenhang stehen, mit befriedigendem Verständnis lesen.

Themenbereich(e):

Umwelt und Gesellschaft

4. Reading: About the guilt felt after shopping

You are going to read a text about the guilt many women feel after shopping. For statements 1-6, choose the answer (True or False) which fits best according to what you read.

About the guilt felt after shopping

According to a recent study, women spend about eight years of their lives shopping. The study was initiated by GE Money and included 3.000 female subjects. Over an estimated period of 63 years, the average woman spends approximately 25.000 hours shopping for food and clothes for both their families and themselves.

The study revealed that a woman makes about 300 shopping trips a year, lasting approximately 340 hours altogether. Considering that shopping for food just to refill the refrigerator and stock the pantry can last up to an hour if the shopping list is long, women spend more than 90 hours in supermarkets every year.

In one year, 90 trips are made to keep their closet up to date. While women go shopping for clothes about 30 times, they go shopping for shoes 15 times, for toiletries 27 times and for accessories 18 times. Buying gifts for friends and family takes up 36 hours every year.

Women do not only go shopping when it is necessary, however. More and more women use shopping to cope with everyday obstacles, emotional problems or stress. Retail therapy is not a myth or something to crack jokes about. There is scientific proof that women, and a growing number of men too, take comfort in spending money when feeling down. The drawback of uncontrolled and unnecessary shopping sprees is that most women feel bad after them.

Women are usually excited and experience joy and satisfaction while shopping. As soon as they are home, looking at all the things they have bought without really needing them and thinking about the amount of money they have spent, a sense of guilt grows inside of them. For those who have to explain their expenses to their partners it might even be worse.

Looking at the numbers, it can be said that eight out of ten women feel bad after a shopping spree. The good mood is quickly followed by guilt and shame. Three quarters of women even start feeling like this while they are still in the shop. Interestingly enough, the guilt felt shortly afterwards does not keep women from continuing their shopping trip. They rather accept that they will have to deal with their negative feelings at a later time.

In today's society it is, however, not easy to resist all those glamorous and tempting things one can buy. Wherever we look we are told that by consuming something we will either look great or feel good. But as long as we do not develop a habit of compulsive shopping, which is actually considered an addiction, going on a shopping spree once in a while should not be a problem.

Prime Time 5. Testen und Fördern, Arbeitsheft (ISBN 978-3-209-08441-5)

1. The study looked at any kind of shopping.

☑ **True**

☐ False

2. Food shopping usually takes an hour.

☐ True

☑ **False**

3. A lot of women are in therapy to overcome their shopping habits.

☐ True

☑ **False**

4. Guilt about shopping grows when other people are involved.

☑ **True**

☐ False

5. The need to go shopping is stronger than the feelings of guilt.

☑ **True**

☐ False

6. Compulsive shopping is considered a less serious addiction.

☐ True

☑ **False**

E8 Reading Strategies
(http://www.uni-klu.ac.at/ltc/downloads/LTC_Technical_Report_2.pdf)

1. **3.2.** Locating, identifying, understanding and comparing facts, opinions, definitions (search reading included).
2. **3.1.** Understanding explicitly stated main idea(s) and/or distinguishing that from supporting details.
3. **3.4.** Understanding cohesive relationships (reference, ellipsis, substitution, conjunction and lexical cohesion).
4. **3.1.** Understanding explicitly stated main idea(s) and/or distinguishing that from supporting details.
5. **3.1.** Understanding explicitly stated main idea(s) and/or distinguishing that from supporting details
6. **3.2.** Locating, identifying, understanding and comparing facts, opinions, definitions (search reading included).

BIST Deskriptoren – LESEN
Die Schülerinnen und Schüler können
einfachen, klar gegliederten Texten zu vertrauten Themen in Zeitungen und Zeitschriften die wesentlichen Informationen entnehmen, wenn sie gegebenenfalls mit visueller Unterstuetzung ausgestattet sind (B1).

GERS Beschreibung – Leseverstehen allgemein
B1 Kann unkomplizierte Sachtexte über Themen, die mit den eigenen Interessen und Fachgebieten in Zusammenhang stehen, mit befriedigendem Verständnis lesen.

Themenbereich(e):
Umwelt und Gesellschaft

Prime Time 5. Testen und Fördern, Arbeitsheft (ISBN 978-3-209-08441-5)

Testen und Fördern

5. Language in use: Fudge

You are going to read a text about how to make fudge. In most lines of the text there is an unnecessary word. Write the unnecessary word in the space provided after each line. Some lines are correct. Indicate these with a tick (✓).

Fudge is a sort of confectionery often flavored up with cocoa, which is	up
famous for its sweetness and richness. When making fudge you have to mix with the	with
following ingredients: milk, butter and sugar. The mixture is then heated on at 116°C,	on
which is also called the 'soft-ball' stage. While cooling, you have to beat it, so that it	✓
will becomes a smooth and creamy substance. If you would like to make chocolate	will
fudge, just add together chocolate to the mixture. Of course, you can also	together
experiment with all sorts of ingredients and from flavors.	from
One of the most more important things about making fudge is getting its texture right.	more
Heating it at the correct temperature is what is necessary for that. It is actually the	✓
temperature that can distinguishes hard caramel from fudge. The higher the top	can
temperature, the more sugar is dissolved and the more water disappears.	✓

6. Language in use: Extraterrestrial life

Complete the text with the words from the list. There are two extra words that you should not use.

belonging	**blessed**	**comes**	**existing**	**going**	**have**
include	**know**	**prove**	**refer**	**search**	**talk**

The word "extraterrestrial" __ ***comes*** __ from the Latin words "extra", which means "not of", and "terrestris", which is "_ ***belonging*** _ to earth". Everything that does not __ ***have*** __ its roots on earth is therefore considered extraterrestrial life.

The various forms of extraterrestrial life __ ***include*** __ bacteria-like organisms as well as human-like beings that are thought to be more sophisticated and advanced than we are. So far we are not in the position to __ ***prove*** __ whether such forms of life exist. Scientists, for example, _ ***search*** _ for evidence of unicellular life __ ***existing*** __ within the Solar System. Regular people most commonly ___ ***talk*** ___ about aliens and the appearance of UFOs when they __ ***refer*** __ to extraterrestrial life. There are, in fact, a lot of people who believe that the Earth can, by no means, be the only planet __ ***blessed*** __ with life.

Not used: going, know

Prime Time 5. Testen und Fördern, Arbeitsheft (ISBN 978-3-209-08441-5)

1. Listening: A casual conversation

You will hear part of a conversation between Angela and Sharon. For questions 1–5, choose the answer which fits best according to what you hear.

1. Where are the two women?

- ☐ in a restaurant
- ☐ in a bar
- ☑ **in a café**

2. Who are the two people talking?

- ☐ students at high school
- ☐ interns at a hospital
- ☑ **freshmen at university**

3. What is Angela studying?

- ☑ **Information Technology**
- ☐ foreign languages
- ☐ medicine

Testen und Fördern

4. Why is the exam mentioned a tough one?

- ☐ Because it is an oral exam.
- ☐ Because the workload is high.
- ☑ **Because the instructor is a problem.**

5. What did Sharon NOT do at the hospital?

- ☐ She took a patient's blood sample.
- ☑ **She signed a prescription.**
- ☐ She put a cast on a patient's leg.

Prime Time 5. Testen und Fördern, Arbeitsheft (ISBN 978-3-209-08441-5)

Tapescript: A casual conversation

Sharon	Oh … May I have another tall soy latte without sugar?
Angela	Make that two!
Waiter	Sure, coming right up. (im Hintergrund sprechend)
Sharon	… So, are you excited about the holidays?
Angela	Definitely! After passing all my finals on Wednesday, I am really looking forward to a short break from studying. After my exit-exam it took me some time to get used to this new environment … which is why the past four months have been really stressful and nerve-wrecking at times. (pause) I can't believe I have actually managed to survive my very first semester at the IT department.
Sharon	I still admire you for that, Angela. Seriously, I couldn't deal with all those programs. Just looking at the screen when you are trying to teach that thing to do what you want it to do, I get all confused … That's why **I** prefer medicine.
Angela	It's not that bad! It's just like learning to speak a foreign language.
Sharon	I've never thought of it that way. Still ... too difficult for me!
Angela	So how are your studies going? Did you finish all your anatomy classes?
Sharon	Most of them. I still have two exams ahead of me; one of them is a really tough one. It's an oral exam and the instructor is weird.
Angela	Hm … What are the requirements?
Sharon	Oh, it's nothing spectacular … just 400 pages I have to cover for only one exam. But from what I've heard, the instructor asks tricky questions, trying to confuse you.
Angela	I'm sure you'll be alright, Sharon! Oh, by the way, how was that first part of your internship at the hospital? Did you get to treat any real patients?
Sharon	They did not want me to take part in any treatments like prescribing medication but I was allowed to watch and, oh, oh … I almost forgot! In the emergency room a doctor asked me to draw a patient's blood and I had to put another patient's leg in a plaster cast. That was kind of exciting. I felt like a real doctor!
Angela	Cool! I am sure you did a great job. Different question! … How about those McDreamys and McSteamys among the doctors? Did you see any?
Sharon	(lachend) Well, let's say TV is a lot better than reality … (lachend)

E8 Listening Strategies

(http://www.uni-klu.ac.at/ltc/downloads/LTC_Technical_Report_3.pdf)

1. **2.3.** Relating utterances to their social and situational contexts.
2. **2.1.** Making inferences and deductions based on information in the text. This can include deducing meaning of unfamiliar lexical items from context.
3. **1.2.** Listening for main idea(s) or important information and distinguishing that from supporting detail or examples. This includes distinguishing fact from opinion when clearly marked.
4. **1.2.** Listening for main idea(s) or important information and distinguishing that from supporting detail or examples. This includes distinguishing fact from opinion when clearly marked.
5. **1.3.** Listening for specific information, including recall of important details. Understanding directions and instructions.

BIST Deskriptoren – HÖREN

Die Schülerinnen und Schüler können

Gesprächen über vertraute Themen die Hauptpunkte entnehmen, wenn Standardsprache verwendet und auch deutlich gesprochen wird (B1).

GERS Beschreibung – Hörverstehen allgemein

B1 Kann die Hauptpunkte verstehen, wenn in deutliche artikulierter Standardsprache über vertraute Dinge gesprochen wird, denen man normalerweise bei der Arbeit, in der Ausbildung oder der Freizeit begegnet; kann auch kurze Erzählungen verstehen.

Themenbereich(e):

Schule und Arbeitswelt

Prime Time 5. Testen und Fördern, Arbeitsheft (ISBN 978-3-209-08441-5)

2. Listening: Music as a means of stress relief

You will hear part of a radio report about how music can help people deal with stress. For statements 1–7, choose the answer (True or False) which fits best according to what you hear.

1. Every form of music can be considered art.

- ☑ **True**
- ☐ False

2. Only people with a certain cultural knowledge enjoy music.

- ☐ True
- ☑ **False**

3. Classical music in particular helps you overcome stress.

- ☐ True
- ☑ **False**

Testen und Fördern

4. Music can completely replace your social contacts.

- ☐ True
- ☑ **False**

5. The melody is as important as the story behind a song.

- ☑ **True**
- ☐ False

6. While listening to music to relax, you should not be disturbed.

- ☑ **True**
- ☐ False

7. This report informs the listeners about the healing power of music.

- ☑ **True**
- ☐ False

Prime Time 5. Testen und Fördern, Arbeitsheft (ISBN 978-3-209-08441-5)

Tapescript: Music as a means of stress relief

Music is with us every single day. You turn on the radio, listen to all sorts of songs and sing along. You come home after a long and exhausting day at school or work and you just switch on your favorite songs, either on your CD player or computer, and drift away.

Music can help us through bad times or make good times even better. It energizes us or makes it easier for us to calm down. Whether it's rock or ballads, up-to-date hits or great and unforgettable oldies, punk or classical music, music is a form of art. Regardless of one's culture or social background, people all over the world love music.

Interestingly, music is not only a plain form of art or a simple means of entertainment. In fact, it is a fantastic means to relieve stress. Recent research has shown that listening to music can help us relax. It helps both, our brain and our nerves to get some rest and to get over the stress and strain we have to deal with every single day.

It is amazing how music can really reduce stress. It is a form of recreation and helps people process whatever they have to cope with in day-to-day life. Listening to music is as valuable as talking to a good friend. Sometimes you have no one to speak with, no one to share your problems, worries or doubts with. Music can also aid in healing. It is either the melody that touches the people or the story behind a song that they can relate to.

When life gets really rough and stresses you out, do not fall into despair. Do not rush things either. Do not necessarily blame other people for the situation you find yourself in. Instead, take a deep breath, turn off your cell phone and your computer – you don't want to get distracted.

Turn on the music you believe will help you relax and forget about everything but yourself. Sit back and allow yourself to tune out. Just let the music do its job and help you and your body to calm down and reflect upon yourself in peace and quiet. Humming along, you will suddenly realize that you feel more balanced, and that your view has changed. It's almost as if you've done this before.

Either way, music is an incredibly precious means of stress relief and relaxation.

E8 Listening Strategies

(http://www.uni-klu.ac.at/ltc/downloads/LTC_Technical_Report_3.pdf)

1. **1.3.** Listening for specific information, including recall of important details. Understanding directions and instructions.
2. **1.3.** Listening for specific information, including recall of important details. Understanding directions and instructions
3. **1.2.** Listening for main idea(s) or important information and distinguishing that from supporting detail or examples. This includes distinguishing fact from opinion when clearly marked.
4. **2.1.** Making inferences and deductions based on information in the text. This can include deducing meaning of unfamiliar lexical items from context.
5. **1.3.** Listening for specific information, including recall of important details. Understanding directions and instructions.
6. **1.2.** Listening for main idea(s) or important information and distinguishing that from supporting detail or examples. This includes distinguishing fact from opinion when clearly marked.
7. **1.1.** Listening for gist.

BIST Deskriptoren – HÖREN

Die Schülerinnen und Schüler können

einfachen Interviews, Berichten, Hörspielen und Sketches zu vertrauten Themen folgen (B1).

GERS Beschreibung – Hörverstehen allgemein

B1 Kann unkomplizierte Sachinformationen über gewöhnliche alltags- oder berufsbezogene Themen verstehen und dabei die Hauptaussagen und Einzelinformationen erkennen, sofern klar artikuliert und mit vertrautem Akzent gesprochen wird.

Themenbereich(e):

Körper und Gesundheit

Prime Time 5. Testen und Fördern, Arbeitsheft (ISBN 978-3-209-08441-5)

3. Reading: Getting about in Greater Bristol

You are going to read a text on a website called *Getting About in Greater Bristol*. For statements 1–6, choose the answer (True, False or Not Given) which fits best according to what you read.

Getting About in Greater Bristol

Getting About in Greater Bristol is a website which provides all sorts of travel information for disabled people wanting to go to Greater Bristol, the area containing and surrounding the city of Bristol in the South West of England. This site has got information on transport for Bath and North East Somerset, Bristol, North Somerset as well as South Gloucestershire.

Due to the influence the Disability Discrimination Act has had on transport, both public transport and places in the Greater Bristol area are constantly being made more accessible.

Since some changes can only be brought about gradually, our website has the aim to help less mobile or disabled people to find their way around the area more easily. It includes recent changes and improvements in access to trains, buses, taxis, community transport services, bus stations, train stations as well as airports. We put a lot of effort in being up to date at all times.

This website introduces people to how to get about in the area using different means of transport and at the same time provides detailed information on transportation that disabled people look for when planning their journeys. Direct links to other sources than transportation and travel websites will make your travel planning even easier.

Finding accommodation suitable for disabled people plays an essential role when making travel arrangements. *Tourism for All* is a national charity and the UK Voice for Accessible Tourism. *Tourism for All* has managed to build up a remarkably good reputation because they have overcome various obstacles or difficulties people with disabilities or older people face when going on a trip. You will find a link to their homepage on our website.

Another link we provide is *Visit Britain*. Regardless of whether you need some practical travel advice or specific information on health insurances or visas, *Visit Britain* can answer your questions. Among other things, it also includes information on British culture.

We are proud to say that England and the Greater Bristol area in particular extend a very warm welcome to disabled visitors and their carers. A lot of public places, including tourist attractions of all sorts, have already been made accessible to people using wheelchairs. Restaurants and hotels have taken all the necessary precautions too.
We will, of course, keep investing our energy and resources in improving our environment for people with disabilities.

◄↑↑

1. *Getting About in Greater Bristol* is a website dedicated to all kinds of tourists.

- ☐ True
- ☑ **False**
- ☐ Not Given

2. Greater Bristol is known for its modern technology in public transport.

- ☐ True
- ☐ False
- ☑ **Not Given**

3. In Greater Bristol, public transport and places could not be made more accessible.

- ☐ True
- ☑ **False**
- ☐ Not Given

4. The website tries to post new developments immediately.

- ☑ **True**
- ☐ False
- ☐ Not Given

◄↑↓

Prime Time 5. Testen und Fördern, Arbeitsheft (ISBN 978-3-209-08441-5)

5. The website also refers people to other transportation websites.

- ☐ True
- ☑ **False**
- ☐ Not Given

6. This text points out a speciality in tourism in the Greater Bristol area.

- ☑ **True**
- ☐ False
- ☐ Not Given

E8 Reading Strategies

(http://www.uni-klu.ac.at/ltc/downloads/LTC_Technical_Report_2.pdf)

1. **3.2.** Locating, identifying, understanding and comparing facts, opinions, definitions (search reading included).
2. **3.2.** Locating, identifying, understanding and comparing facts, opinions, definitions (search reading included).
3. **3.1.** Understanding explicitly stated main idea(s) and/or distinguishing that from supporting details.
4. **3.1.** Understanding explicitly stated main idea(s) and/or distinguishing that from supporting details.
5. **3.2.** Locating, identifying, understanding and comparing facts, opinions, definitions (search reading included).
6. **1.3.** Identifying text purpose.

BIST Deskriptoren – LESEN

Die Schülerinnen und Schüler können

einfachen, klar gegliederten Texten zu vertrauten Themen in Zeitungen und Zeitschriften die wesentlichen Informationen entnehmen, wenn sie gegebenenfalls mit visueller Unterstützung ausgestattet sind (B1).

GERS Beschreibung – Leseverstehen allgemein

B1 Kann unkomplizierte Sachtexte über Themen, die mit den eigenen Interessen und Fachgebieten in Zusammenhang stehen, mit befriedigendem Verständnis lesen.

Themenbereich(e):

Umwelt und Gesellschaft

Prime Time 5. Testen und Fördern, Arbeitsheft (ISBN 978-3-209-08441-5)

4. Reading: Excessive use of media in teenagers

You are going to read a text on excessive use of media in teenagers. For questions 1–5, choose the answer which fits best according to what you read.

Excessive use of media in teenagers

Children and teenagers say that they are in full control of the amount of time they spend using all sorts of media and that they would be able to stop media consumption at any time. However, more and more young people are overwhelmed with the great variety of media-related input they are confronted with every day. They frequently do not even realize any more how many hours they spend playing video games, chatting with their friends on the phone, updating their profiles on social networking sites or just watching TV.

A lot of parents get the impression that their children are addicted to media consumption, which is an alarming fact. In the past few years, it has been observed that media replace essential activities in young people's lives, ranging from the replacement of physical activity and homework to the replacement of important personal relationships. If this is the case, parents need to set up easy and clear rules and try to change their children's behavior.

Media and the body

Most of the media young people consume ask for sitting. They either sit in front of the TV on the couch or in front of their computer screen on a chair or they might even lie in bed sending text messages to their friends while having their notebooks sitting on their laps. Either way, young people are generally more sedentary when consuming media, except for those listening to their iPods while jogging or doing their workout on an exercise bike.

What is even worse than just sitting is the fact that most young people take in a lot of unhealthy food while sitting. Consuming junk food frequently goes hand in hand with consuming media. If there is no exercise whatsoever, the circumstances mentioned above can quickly lead to weight gain and other physical problems.

Media and homework

Many young people are so extremely absorbed in whatever kind of media they are using that they do not feel time passing. It is the entertainment and excitement they experience when playing games or communicating with peers via the phone or Internet that makes them forget everything else, their homework included. While this may have an immediate negative effect on their marks, they also miss out on a lot of personal development and growth.

Testen und Fördern

Media and relationships

The effects excessive media consumption can have are twofold. On the one hand, it can lead to complete isolation. Young people might turn away from family and friends because there is no time for personal interaction due to the time spent making one's way to all the levels in a video game, for example. On the other hand, there might be over-communication. Today, people can play video games online together with other people. They are communicating with each other all the time, but unfortunately not in person. While this certainly is some sort of interaction, it is not one that promotes the development of good social skills.

If parents have children who fit that pattern, they need to take the situation at home seriously and do something about it. As a first step, parents and children need to sit down together and discuss possible changes in the children's media usage habits. Setting up strict rules that do not make much sense, like forbidding media consumption altogether, is the wrong thing to do. Instead, parents should build on the suggestions their children have and work out a good and fair set of rules together.

1. What does 'are overwhelmed with' in the first paragraph mean?

☐ to be in control of

☑ **to be flooded with**

☐ to be excited about

2. How do teenagers compensate for their lack of exercise when consuming media?

☐ They consume a lot of healthy food.

☐ They do a lot of sports.

☑ **They often do not compensate for it.**

Prime Time 5. Testen und Fördern, Arbeitsheft (ISBN 978-3-209-08441-5)

3. Why do teenagers frequently not do their homework?

- ☐ They are not interested in doing it.
- ☑ **They do not have enough time for it.**
- ☐ They do not think it affects their marks.

4. How does the writer of the text see online communication?

- ☐ It is a good way to communicate with more people at the same time.
- ☐ In combination with real-life, people are communicating too much.
- ☑ **It has a negative influence on people's communication skills.**

5. How should parents react to excessive media usage?

- ☑ **They should take their children's opinions seriously.**
- ☐ They should change their own media usage habits.
- ☐ They should present their children with strict rules.

E8 Reading Strategies

(http://www.uni-klu.ac.at/ltc/downloads/LTC_Technical_Report_2.pdf)

1. **4.1.** Predicting the meaning of (unknown) words from the context.
2. **3.5.** Making propositional inferences (deducing information that is not explicitly stated from information that is explicitly stated).
3. **3.1.** Understanding explicitly stated main idea(s) and/or distinguishing that from supporting details.
4. **3.2.** Locating, identifying, understanding and comparing facts, opinions, definitions (search reading included).
5. **3.1.** Understanding explicitly stated main idea(s) and/or distinguishing that from supporting details.

BIST Deskriptoren – LESEN

Die Schülerinnen und Schüler können
unkomplizierte Sachtexte über Themen, die mit den eigenen Interessen und Fachgebieten aus den Themenbereichen des Lehrplans in Zusammenhang stehen, mit befriedigendem Verständnis lesen (B1).

GERS Beschreibung – Leseverstehen allgemein

B1 Kann unkomplizierte Sachtexte über Themen, die mit den eigenen Interessen und Fachgebieten in Zusammenhang stehen, mit befriedigendem Verständnis lesen.

Themenbereich(e):

Umwelt und Gesellschaft

5. Language in use: Google

You are going to read a text about Google. In most lines of the text there is an unnecessary word. Write the unnecessary word in the space provided after each line. Some lines are correct. Indicate these with a tick (✓).

Google is an American multinational public corporation. It also operates in the fields	also
of Internet search, from advertising technologies and cloud computing, which is	from
Internet-based computing.	✓
Sergey Brin and Larry Page, who also known as the 'Google Guys', founded the	who
company in 1998. Its initial public offering took place in 2004. Their headquarters	✓
are in around Mountain View, California, where they have been since 2006. The	around
company's mission statement has always been to make all the information available	✓
in the world to accessible to everybody.	to
While the company's core is its web and search engine, Google now offers a wide	and
variety of applications and from tools, ranging from online productivity software like	from
Gmail and social networking tools like Google Buzz to the web browser Google	✓
Chrome or as the service Google Books.	as
Google Search, Google's web search engine, is still being the company's most popular	being
service. In the United States alone, Google is the dominant search engine only,	only
holding a market share of approximately 66%.	✓

◄ ↓ ↔

6. Language in use: Stand-up comedy

Read the text on stand-up comedy. Some words are missing. Use the words in brackets to form words that fit in the gaps. Write your answers in the gaps.

Stand-up comedy is a particular kind of comedy in which the comedian is on stage, performing in front of a live audience, (1) generally (**general**) speaking directly to them and (2) involving (**involve**) them in his act. High-profile comedians are often filmed during their (3) performances (**perform**) so that their shows can be made available via DVD, television or the Internet.

The person standing on stage is (4) referred (**refer**) to as "stand-up comedian", "comic" or just "stand-up".

Stand-up performances are generally fairly short and are (5) characterised (**characterise**) by short jokes, one-liners and (6) humorous (**humour**) stories which are presented one after the other without much (7) interruption (**interrupt**).

There are stand-ups who use music or magic tricks to spice up their performances. The performances themselves usually take place in comedy clubs and bars or colleges and theatres.

Being (8) successful (**success**) as a stand-up comedian is the result of hard work. Very often comedians work (9) incredibly (**incredible**) long for very short programmes, which they keep improving while repeatedly performing them on stage.

◄ ↓ ↕

Prime Time 5. Testen und Fördern, Arbeitsheft (ISBN 978-3-209-08441-5)

Testen und Fördern

7. Writing: Reality TV shows (Short text)

BIST Deskriptoren – SCHREIBEN

Die Schülerinnen und Schüler können

Erfahrungsberichte schreiben, in denen Gefühle und Reaktionen in einem einfachen, zusammenhängenden Text wiedergegeben werden (B1).

GERS Beschreibung – SCHREIBEN

B1 Kann unkomplizierte Sachtexte über Themen, die mit den eigenen Interessen und Fachgebieten in Zusammenhang stehen, mit befriedigendem Verständnis lesen.

Themenbereich(e):

Kultur, Medien und Literatur

Prime Time 5. Testen und Fördern, Arbeitsheft (ISBN 978-3-209-08441-5)

Testen und Fördern

1. Listening: Facebook

You will hear a discussion between two students about Facebook. For statements 1–6, choose the answer (True or False) which fits best according to what you hear.

1. This is the second discussion taking place this week.

- ☐ True
- ☑ **False**

2. Today millions of users must use Facebook.

- ☐ True
- ☑ **False**

3. Simon thinks Facebook is the best social platform.

- ☐ True
- ☑ **False**

Testen und Fördern

4. Lisa is not against online communication.

- ☑ **True**
- ☐ False

5. Simon argues that the owners of Facebook are not allowed to keep personal information.

- ☐ True
- ☑ **False**

6. Many people use Facebook to avoid going out.

- ☑ **True**
- ☐ False

Prime Time 5. Testen und Fördern, Arbeitsheft (ISBN 978-3-209-08441-5)

Tapescript: Facebook

Teacher	Good morning everybody! I think today Simon and Lisa are up for this week's discussion. (Pause) Simon … Lisa! Would you please take a seat out here. (Klassengeraeusche) If I remember correctly, you are going to discuss the positive and negative aspects of Facebook.
Simon	Yes … Good morning! Lisa and I have decided to talk about Facebook because social networking sites are becoming more and more significant for masses of people. (Pause) At the moment Facebook has got 500 million users and there are many, many teenagers among them, which is also a reason why we have chosen this topic. I am going to represent the supporters of Facebook …
Lisa	… and I am going to speak for the opponents. (auffordernd) Simon!
Simon	One of the best things about Facebook and any other social platforms is that you can share ideas, moods and pictures with your friends any time you feel like it. You can either post comments, update your status or use chat rooms to stay in touch with your buddies.
Lisa	I agree that today communication is a lot easier because of the internet. When it comes to Facebook I would not consider every post necessary. Let me give you an example! Who is interested in reading about what you had for lunch or for how long you have been waiting for the bus. I don't believe that anybody's life is that important!
Simon	But this is what social contact is all about. In real-life conversations people **also** say things that are unimportant or even stupid.
Lisa	That may be true, but don't forget that real-life conversations happen in real time. As soon as something is said, it's gone again. If you post a stupid comment online, it will be there forever.
Simon	But you can delete your posts, too.
Lisa	That's an illusion. The people who own Facebook keep everything.
Simon	They may keep all the data but they are not permitted to pass that information on to others … (Pause) Another positive aspect of Facebook is that it offers many ways to entertain yourself. You can play hundreds of games like Farmville, do fun quizzes, look at photos that other people have posted or link your page to youtube clips.
Lisa	I would not necessarily see that as something positive. Facebook is just another excuse for not going outside and meeting other people. I am sure you have already heard about lots of teenagers and adults who have become addicted and pulled back from their social contacts.
Teacher	Lisa, Simon. Thank you for making such great points. It's time for class discussion. (fade out)

◄↓↓

E8 Listening Strategies

(http://www.uni-klu.ac.at/ltc/downloads/LTC_Technical_Report_3.pdf)

1. **2.1.** Making inferences and deductions based on information in the text. This can include deducing meaning of unfamiliar lexical items from context.
2. **1.2.** Listening for main idea(s) or important information and distinguishing that from supporting detail or examples. This includes distinguishing fact from opinion when clearly marked.
3. **1.3.** Listening for specific information, including recall of important details. Understanding directions and instructions.
4. **2.2.** Determining a speaker's attitude or intention towards a listener or a topic.
5. **1.3.** Listening for specific information, including recall of important details. Understanding directions and instructions.
6. **1.3.** Listening for specific information, including recall of important details. Understanding directions and instructions.

BIST Deskriptoren – HÖREN

Die Schülerinnen und Schüler können

Gesprächen über vertraute Themen die Hauptpunkte entnehmen, wenn Standardsprache verwendet und auch deutlich gesprochen wird (B1).

GERS Beschreibung – Hörverstehen allgemein

B1 Kann die Hauptpunkte verstehen, wenn in deutliche artikulierter Standardsprache über vertraute Dinge gesprochen wird, denen man normalerweise bei der Arbeit, in der Ausbildung oder der Freizeit begegnet; kann auch kurze Erzählungen verstehen.

Themenbereich(e):

Hobbys und Interessen

◄↓↓

Prime Time 5. Testen und Fördern, Arbeitsheft (ISBN 978-3-209-08441-5)

2. Listening: Greek-Americans

You will hear part of a radio report about Greek-Americans. For questions 1–5, choose the answer which fits best according to what you hear.

1. Which of the following is the main religion in Greece?

- ☐ the Roman Catholic Church
- ☑ **the Eastern Orthodox Church**
- ☐ the Greek Catholic Church

2. When did the first Greek arrive in America?

- ☑ **in the 16th century**
- ☐ in the 18th century
- ☐ in the 19th century

3. Why did many Greeks leave their home country?

- ☐ because of religious persecution
- ☐ because of poor living conditions
- ☑ **because of the economy**

Testen und Fördern

4. What kind of business did most Greeks in Tarpon Springs work in?

- ☐ sponge selling
- ☑ **sponge diving**
- ☐ sponge manufacturing

5. What is the purpose of this report?

- ☑ **to inform the listeners about the Greek-Americans' lifestyle**
- ☐ to criticize the Greek-Americans' way of living
- ☐ to persuade the listeners to visit Tarpon Springs

Prime Time 5. Testen und Fördern, Arbeitsheft (ISBN 978-3-209-08441-5)

Tapescript: Greek-Americans

Welcome to *Around the U.S.* This is Lou Zima and today we are taking a closer look at the Greek part of our country's magnificent mosaic.

Officially known as the Hellenic Republic, Greece is a European country on the southern end of the Balkan Peninsula between the Aegean and Mediterranean Seas. Its neighboring countries are Albania, the Republic of Macedonia, Bulgaria and Turkey, and the capital city is Athens.

Greece has a total population of about ten million, and can be considered a linguistically and ethnically homogeneous nation, with 97% of the people speaking Greek. Most people belong to the Eastern Orthodox Church. Only a small percentage of the people living in Greece are Muslim, Roman Catholic, Greek Catholic, or Jewish.

Official records confirm that the Greek sailor Don Teodoro or Theodoros was the first Greek to set foot on America in 1528. One of the first Greek colonies was to be found near Saint Augustine, Florida, and set up in the 18th century. While the colony itself was a failure, many Greeks coming to America because of the colony had already moved elsewhere and were successful as merchants and businessmen. Until the 1880s, the U.S. Greek population was relatively small. However, at the beginning of the 20th century, poor economic conditions in Greece made many people leave their country and immigrate to the United States. There they hoped to make a fortune, while still wishing to return back home some day.

Although some Greeks started settling in the Northeast as well as the Midwest of the United States, most Greeks were to be found in Tarpon Springs, Florida, where they started an incredibly successful sponge diving business. Today, Tarpon Springs still has the highest percentage of Greek-Americans in the U.S. and calls itself the "sponge" capital of the world.

Tarpon Springs is unique from its restaurants to its monuments because the Greeks living there are extremely keen on preserving their traditions and beliefs. The role of family and the church as well as the way they harvest the sponges have all been kept alive in Tarpon Springs for more than four generations. While many aspects of their lives have remained, traditional Greek-Americans' work ethics are distinctly modern.

This is Lou Zima and you are listening to *Around the U.S.* And I'll be back with more on Greek-Americans in New York and Chicago in a few minutes.

E8 Listening Strategies

(http://www.uni-klu.ac.at/ltc/downloads/LTC_Technical_Report_3.pdf)

1. **1.3.** Listening for specific information, including recall of important details. Understanding directions and instructions.
2. **1.2.** Listening for main idea(s) or important information and distinguishing that from supporting detail or examples. This includes distinguishing fact from opinion when clearly marked.
3. **1.3.** Listening for specific information, including recall of important details. Understanding directions and instructions.
4. **1.3.** Listening for specific information, including recall of important details. Understanding directions and instructions.
5. **1.1.** Listening for gist.

BIST Deskriptoren – HÖREN

Die Schülerinnen und Schüler können

einfachen Interviews, Berichten, Hörspielen und Sketches zu vertrauten Themen folgen (B1).

GERS Beschreibung – Hörverstehen allgemein

B1 Kann unkomplizierte Sachinformationen über gewöhnliche alltags- oder berufsbezogene Themen verstehen und dabei die Hauptaussagen und Einzelinformationen erkennen, sofern klar artikuliert und mit vertrautem Akzent gesprochen wird.

Themenbereich(e):

Interkulturelle und landeskundliche Aspekte

Prime Time 5. Testen und Fördern, Arbeitsheft (ISBN 978-3-209-08441-5)

3. Reading: The trouble with boys in school

You are going to read a text on the trouble with boys in school. For questions 1–5, choose the answer which fits best according to what you read.

The trouble with boys in school

This is to comment on the lecture my classmates and I listened to at school today. Peg Tyre, an acclaimed American journalist and writer, presented her book 'The Trouble With Boys' in our assembly hall today.

She started out by telling us about a 16-year-old boy who seems to be a very bright, thoughtful and nice teenager when talking to him outside of school. His relationship with his parents is a very good one. He likes rock music and plays the guitar regularly. However, as soon as he enters his school building in Salt Lake City he gets extremely nervous and puts on a fearful look. In class, he quickly loses focus and therefore often misses important information. His teachers do not have the time to explain things twice because they have to deal with approximately 36 students per class, and he has already been classified as stupid and lazy even though he can perform excellently when not put under pressure.

According to Peg Tyre, this boy's description fits a lot of young boys today. Statistics say that more and more boys are falling behind in our school system. In elementary school, for example, boys are two times more likely to be diagnosed with learning disabilities than girls. In higher classes, the problems continue with boys falling behind with regard to standardized writing tests, just to mention one aspect. Statistics also show that the number of boys disliking school has risen about 71% in the past 30 years. As far as the future is concerned, Tyre does not believe that the gap between boys and girls will close soon.

I can only confirm that boys tend to get lower grades than girls. The reasons for this vary, of course. One might be that both students and teachers act under a lot of pressure nowadays. There are states in the US in which teachers do not really have a say in when and how they will teach their students certain things. Quite on the contrary, teachers are told by the state what, when and how to teach, leaving the students' abilities totally out of consideration. The standardized tests students have to take do not allow for a lot of time to process the materials students are presented with every single day. It is basically about memorizing one fact after the other, without ever asking what they think about these facts.

Another reason I believe to be responsible for the boys' lower achievement is that in many cases boys are asked to behave like girls. They are told to sit still, focus and just be quiet. There is not much room for running around, screaming or just letting off some steam. Sports classes have even been cut in favor of more theory-based subjects.

One more thing that I consider important is that more and more boys do not like reading. The media we have access to make it easy to find something other to do than read. While girls seem to like reading, boys often think of it as something unmanly, which, of course, is not true. I prefer ending my day with a book, but my friends do not necessarily know that because they would rather play soccer or hit the town.

To sum it up, I have to say that I enjoyed listening to Peg Tyre. The statistics and stories she presented were very interesting and shocking at the same time. I hope that politicians, educators, teachers and parents will soon figure out a way to put the boys in this country back on track because they deserve a fair chance in life.

Testen und Fördern

1. Why did Peg Tyre start her lecture with the example of a 16-year-old boy?

- ☐ to illustrate why teachers do not have time to repeat information
- ☑ **to illustrate in what ways teenage boys react to school**
- ☐ to illustrate the influence of the parents on teenage boys

2. Why do boys fall behind at school?

- ☐ Because the structure of writing tests has changed.
- ☐ Because they are not interested in school.
- ☑ **Because they have difficulties studying.**

3. What does the writer criticize about the school system?

- ☑ **The states have too much influence on the information presented.**
- ☐ The teachers do not care about what the students are interested in.
- ☐ The students are presented with too much detailed information.

4. What is the writer's attitude towards reading?

- ☐ He knows reading is important but thinks only girls should do it.
- ☐ He sometimes reads but prefers doing sports or going out.
- ☑ **He likes reading but tries to hide it from his friends.**

5. What sort of text is this?

- ☑ **personal statement**
- ☐ descriptive essay
- ☐ formal letter

Prime Time 5. Testen und Fördern, Arbeitsheft (ISBN 978-3-209-08441-5)

4. Reading: Meg comes to see me in Aussie Land!

You are going to read a blog entry written by Karen, who is currently in Australia. For statements 1–7, choose the answer (True or False) which fits best according to what you read.

This goes to my dearest friends and all my faithful readers! I hereby sincerely apologize for not posting anything in the last two weeks, which is usually so not me but I simply couldn't find the time to do so because … Can you believe it?! My best friend Meg came to see me in the land of Aussies and stayed for almost twelve days! The time we spent together was so exciting and packed with fun, laughter, and unforgettable experiences! I hope you can forgive me ☺
Ok, back to the story!
Meg arrived in Brisbane on July 3. I was so excited about her arrival even days before I actually saw her again after – what seemed to me like – an eternity!
On her arrival day we did nothing but have coffee and talk about everything that was new with her.
The first three days we only spent around Brisbane. I was busy showing her the ins and outs of this great city while she was trying to keep up with soaking in all the beauty this place has to offer. We even got round to meeting my new friends on campus. They seemed to like each other, which I find cool.
Apart from eating the most delicious food in some of the smaller restaurants and bars in Brisbane and doing excessive shopping once or twice, we just had the best time doing nothing but laughing our heads off.
On Meg's fourth day in Australia we went to Cairns, which is very close to the Great Barrier Reef, a fantastic place for scuba diving, snorkeling and reef cruising. After having a very tasty breakfast in a cute little café, we decided to lie out in the grass a little since you won't find beaches in Cairns. I swear … we only lay there for an hour! You wouldn't believe what 1 hour of Aussie sun can do to your body. Looking in the mirror back in the hotel we couldn't believe our eyes: We were roasted!!! Meg started to laugh hysterically and called me a lobster! ☺
The next day we were headed to the Great Barrier Reef. Meg desperately wanted to go there, which was fine by me since I love the GBR.
While snorkeling on various reefs we saw so many different kinds of coral and fish. You wouldn't believe the variety of beautiful and colorful fish you get so see there. What's even better is the water! It's crystal clear!!! Just like in the movies!
Time flew when Meg was with me. If I wrote down everything that we did, it would probably take me hours, which I don't have because class starts in about 50 minutes.
There is just one more thing we did that I would like to share with you because it was great fun. One day we went to Steve Irwin Australia Zoo, north of Brisbane. I had wanted to go there all semester and I figured it was even better to go there with my best friend. We got to play with some kangaroos and koalas. The little koala babies in the animal hospital were the cutest thing in the world I have ever seen. We felt like cuddling them and taking them home with us. Our zoo day was just an awesome day!
Oh, it's late. I have to run …
You all know that I am having a great time here in Brissy but I also miss my family and friends a lot. It's only another four weeks and I will get to go back home! Can't wait to see you all again!
Love, Karen

Testen und Fördern

E8 Reading Strategies

(http://www.uni-klu.ac.at/ltc/downloads/LTC_Technical_Report_2.pdf)

1. **3.5.** Making propositional inferences (deducing information that is not explicitly stated from information that is explicitly stated).
2. **3.2.** Locating, identifying, understanding and comparing facts, opinions, definitions (search reading included).
3. **3.2.** Locating, identifying, understanding and comparing facts, opinions, definitions (search reading included).
4. **3.5.** Making propositional inferences (deducing information that is not explicitly stated from information that is explicitly stated).
5. **1.1.** Identifying text type

BIST Deskriptoren – LESEN

Die Schülerinnen und Schüler können
unkomplizierte Sachtexte über Themen, die mit den eigenen Interessen und Fachgebieten aus den Themenbereichen des Lehrplans in Zusammenhang stehen, mit befriedigendem Verständnis lesen (B1).

GERS Beschreibung – Leseverstehen allgemein

B1 Kann unkomplizierte Sachtexte über Themen, die mit den eigenen Interessen und Fachgebieten in Zusammenhang stehen, mit befriedigendem Verständnis lesen.

Themenbereich(e):

Schule und Arbeitswelt

Prime Time 5. Testen und Fördern, Arbeitsheft (ISBN 978-3-209-08441-5)

Testen und Fördern

1. Karen cares about updating her friends at home.

☑ True
☐ False

2. On Meg's first day in Brisbane the girls talked about what had been going on in both their lives.

☐ True
☑ False

3. Karen is glad Meg and her Aussie friends got along well.

☑ True
☐ False

4. The first days were full of exciting trips.

☐ True
☑ False

5. The girls got sunburned while snorkeling the Great Barrier Reef.

☐ True
☑ False

6. Karen has tried to include everything in her blog that she and Meg did.

☐ True
☑ False

7. Karen will leave Brisbane in not more than four weeks.

☑ True
☐ False

Testen und Fördern

E8 Reading Strategies

(http://www.uni-klu.ac.at/ltc/downloads/LTC_Technical_Report_2.pdf)

1. **3.1.** Understanding explicitly stated main idea(s) and/or distinguishing that from supporting details.
2. **3.2.** Locating, identifying, understanding and comparing facts, opinions, definitions (search reading included).
3. **3.1.** Understanding explicitly stated main idea(s) and/or distinguishing that from supporting details.
4. **3.2.** Locating, identifying, understanding and comparing facts, opinions, definitions (search reading included).
5. **2.1.** Finding specific details (e.g. names, figures, dates, any other surface-level information).
6. **3.2.** Locating, identifying, understanding and comparing facts, opinions, definitions (search reading included).
7. **3.1.** Understanding explicitly stated main idea(s) and/or distinguishing that from supporting details.

BIST Deskriptoren – LESEN

Die Schülerinnen und Schüler können

einfachen, klar gegliederten Texten zu vertrauten Themen in Zeitungen und Zeitschriften die wesentlichen Informationen entnehmen, wenn sie gegebenenfalls mit visueller Unterstützung ausgestattet sind (B1).

GERS Beschreibung – Leseverstehen allgemein

B1 Kann unkomplizierte Sachtexte über Themen, die mit den eigenen Interessen und Fachgebieten in Zusammenhang stehen, mit befriedigendem Verständnis lesen.

Themenbereich(e):

Erlebnisse und Fantasiewelt

Prime Time 5. Testen und Fördern, Arbeitsheft (ISBN 978-3-209-08441-5)

Testen und Fördern

5. Language in use: Airplanes and environmental concerns

Read through the text and choose the correct answer (A or B) for each gap (1–9) in the text.

One of the consequences of global economic growth is the (1) ….. increase in air travel. While airlines are (2) ….. satisfied with the steadily growing numbers of passengers taking to the skies and the transportation taken care of via airplanes, there are at the same time more and more (3) ….. concerns.

Airplane emissions have been identified as (4) ….. contributing to the greenhouse effect and therefore to climate change. Experts expect a (5) ….. 50% rise in carbon dioxide emissions by the middle of the 21st century. Compared to cars, the (6) ….. emissions coming from airplanes contribute to climate change three times as much because planes emit their gases (7) ….. in the atmosphere.

(8) ….., the Kyoto Protocol, an international agreement on climate change, does not set any restrictions on carbon dioxide emissions caused by air travel, although planes are (9) ….. for emitting 600 million tons of CO_2 every year.

(1) **A constant** B constantly
(2) A incredible **B incredibly**
(3) **A environmental** B environmentally
(4) A critical **B critically**
(5) **A dramatic** B dramatically
(6) **A enormous** B enormously
(7) **A high** B highly
(8) A Interesting **B Interestingly**
(9) **A responsible** B responsibly

Testen und Fördern

6. Language in use: Eating healthy food

Complete the text with the words from the list. There are two extra words that you should not use.

are – are made – comes – cutting – do – do not – is – need – think – will realize

When it (1) **comes** to eating healthy food, a lot of people (2) **think** that this means eating food that does not taste good or look nice. What they immediately think about are Brussels sprouts, cauliflower, goat cheese or tofu, when in fact healthy food (3) **is** much more than that. It is basically about eating enough fruits, vegetables, oily fish and whole grain foods while (4) **cutting** back on things like red meat, sugary drinks and refined grains.

A healthy diet is about keeping the balance. If you (5) **are** willing to experiment a little, you (6) **will realize** how exciting, tasty and exotic other kinds of food can be.

There is one myth you should bear in mind! Vegetarian dishes are not always healthier than non-vegetarian dishes. There are quite a few vegetarian dishes that (7) **are made** with lots of oil, sauces and cheese. They are also often fried, which is why they (8) **do not** always qualify as healthy dishes.

Distractors: do, need

Prime Time 5. Testen und Fördern, Arbeitsheft (ISBN 978-3-209-08441-5)

7. Writing: The upset passenger (E-mail)

BIST Deskriptoren – SCHREIBEN

Die Schülerinnen und Schüler können

Erfahrungsberichte schreiben, in denen Gefühle und Reaktionen in einem einfachen, zusammenhängenden Text wiedergegeben werden (B1).

GERS Beschreibung – SCHREIBEN

B1 Kann unkomplizierte Sachtexte über Themen, die mit den eigenen Interessen und Fachgebieten in Zusammenhang stehen, mit befriedigendem Verständnis lesen.

Themenbereich(e):

Erlebnisse und Fantasiewelt

Prime Time 5. Testen und Fördern, Arbeitsheft (ISBN 978-3-209-08441-5)